# How to Survive in the 21st Century

# How to Survive in the 21st Century

Herbert E. Douglass

REVIEW AND HERALD® PUBLISHING ASSOCIATION
HAGERSTOWN, MD 21740

The author assumes full responsibility for the accuracy of all facts and quotations as cited in this book



This book was
Edited by Raymond H. Woolsey
Copyedited by Delma Miller and James Cavil
Designed by Emily Harding
Cover designed by GenesisDesign/Bryan Gray
Electronic makup by Shirley M. Bolivar
Typeset: 11/13 Bembo

PRINTED IN U.S.A.

04 03 02 01 00 5 4 3 2 1

**R&H Cataloging Service**
Douglass, Herbert E. 1927-
How to survive in the 21st century.
1. Eschatology. 2. End of the world. I. Title

236

ISBN 0-8280-1423-X

# CONTENTS

Chapter One

# A Few First Words . . .

As I write, racing toward me at the rate of 3,600 seconds per hour is that magic moment when the cosmic odometer turns over to show three zeros—for the second time in the Christian Era: A.D. 2000, or Y2K. In popular thinking, a new year, a new decade, a new century, a new millennium—a quadruple blast from Father Time!

More than 1,000 companies have requested trademarks to use the word "millennium" in names or slogans for products ranging from vitamins to pet foods to fishing tackle. That's four times more than the U.S. Patent and Trademark Office had for Desert Storm, the next most popular trademark. General Mills has its Millennium Crunch. M&Ms are the "official" millennium candy.

We can buy nonstick cookware for the ages—Farberware Millennium. Chrysler Motors named its concept car the "Millennium." Fidelity Investments has a mutual fund called The New Millennium. In San Francisco you can eat in one of the Bay Area's finest restaurants, Millennium, where elegant vegetarian dining is not an oxymoron. In England Her Majesty's government appointed a "Millennium Commission"; one of its projects to celebrate MM (2000) will be a gigantic ferris wheel looming 200 feet high, above Big Ben and the House of Parliament.

On we could go, adding to the excitement of Y2K, or MM (2000). But this book is like no other book about the millennium. I will not try to scare you with crashing asteroids or aliens from outer space. Nor will I attempt to frighten you with bar codes embedded in your hand or forehead so that the antichrist or 666 will control your every move and thought—although we will talk about that.

On the other hand, I will not anesthetize you with carefree optimism that does not see beyond the incredible breakthroughs in the research laboratories of medical science, space and energy technology, and computerized agriculture and communication—although we will review these awesome wonders as well.

One fact remains constant: In our fast-moving world, far faster than any period in human history, only certain people will survive with their health, peace, and hope in the future intact. Most people will become increasingly frustrated, resentful, and angry. Evidence of this simple fact is the astounding sales of Prozac on one hand, and on the other, the new and scary behavior we call "road rage." Or in the speechless breakdown of civilized conduct among the young—randomly killing schoolmates and teachers as coolly as eating a sandwich. Or the amazing growing rash of incivilities in the workplace, where a new category of terms have been "invented" in recent months, such as counterproductive behavior, workplace aggression, personality conflict, workplace mistreatment, interpersonal deviance, bullying, plus the deadly duels over parking spaces!

Further signals of a coming storm that this world has seen only once before come from the dreary but rising statistics of teen suicides. Many are worried that while leading economic indicators continue to rise, the moral, cultural, and social indicators are sinking into new lows.

### Flawed Human Predictions

Although we may note some "predictions" of experts, we will not emphasize them. Human knowledge of the future is extremely limited, sometimes simply farcical. In 1960 world leaders were asked how things would be in the year 2000. Israeli prime minister David Ben-Gurion predicted that the Soviet Union would be transformed into a "free and democratic country," and that there would be peace between Arabs and Israelis.

Going back further, in 1899 Charles H. Duell, the U.S. commissioner of patents, urged President McKinley to abolish his office because "everything that can be invented has been invented."* Henry Ford's lawyer was advised by a bank president in 1903 not to invest in the Ford Motor Company because "the horse is here to stay, but the automobile is only a novelty, a fad." Marshal Ferdinand Foch, military strategist and future commander of French forces in

World War I, said in 1911: "Airplanes are interesting toys but of no military value."

In 1922 Joseph Daniels, U.S. secretary of the Navy, said that the Japanese fleet could never be able to "deal an unexpected flow on our Pacific possessions. . . . Radio makes surprise impossible." On December 4, 1941, Frank Knox, secretary of the Navy, calmed his country: "No matter what happens, the U.S. Navy is not going to be caught napping." (Pearl Harbor was attacked three days later.) In 1927 the head of Warner Brothers Pictures, Harry M. Warner, ridiculed the idea that anyone would want "to hear actors talking." Yale University professor of economics Irving Fisher observed in 1929 that "stocks have reached what looks like a permanently high plateau."

British prime minister Lloyd George assured the world in 1934, "Believe me, Germany is unable to wage war." In 1946 Darryl F. Zanuck, head of Twentieth Century Fox, declared: "Television won't be able to hold on to any market it captures after the first six months. People will soon get tired of staring at a plywood box every night." In a similar vein, the leadership of Decca Records rejected the Beatles in 1962, saying, "We don't like their sound. Groups of guitars are on the way out."

Lee DeForest, often called the father of radio, predicted that "man will never reach the moon regardless of all future scientific advances." The founder and president of Digital Equipment, Ken Olsen, may take the prize in missing the future. In 1977 he stated, "There is no reason for any individual to have a computer in their home."

But this book is not about predictions, even those uttered by knowledgeable men and women. *This book is about you—the survivor who chooses not to live in moral and cultural decadence, or to be chained to a body that limps and drags into "modern maturity."* In the face of incredible change, where your high school and college skills may not seem to be adequate for the rapidly changing job market, when the majority of the world's population would rather watch either gory or sleazy TV programs or home videos, when it seems for most that character does not matter—you, *you,* don't have to be caught in the current of meaninglessness. Only certain people will swim and survive. You can be a survivor!

In this book we will consider the survivor's perspective as he or she looks at 2000 and beyond. Survivors keep their eyes on reality, not merely on front-page stories or the latest psychobabble that hypnotizes so many who want to believe in something, anything, as long as it is exciting or mysterious enough. Survivors are realists, not merely pessimistic or optimistic.

Because survivors are realists, they prepare for crises, for the unknown. Why do only certain people survive the big crises or the overwhelming surprises? I will outline how you can prepare physically, mentally, morally, and spiritually for the predictable crises already building and speeding toward us. Tomorrow is not for the weak!

I want you to take the long view and see the big picture. Survivors do not permit themselves to be lost in insignificance. They survive because they sense meaning amidst chaos, when life seems to tumble in.

In fact, they know that God has laid out a survival plan for all of us, especially for those who live in these hectic days that some are calling the "end times."

So let us begin by checking out how survivors think and respond to reality as the future races toward them. We need all the help we can get today so that we will be happy survivors in 2000 *and beyond!*

---

*This and the following incidents and quotations may be found in Christopher Cerf and Victor Navasky, *The Experts Speak* (New York: Villard, 1998).

# Chapter Two

# Survivors Are Realists, Not Pessimists

Survivors are realists; they know the territory ahead. Of course, survivors cannot predict the future any more than anyone else. Yet they are prepared for it. In some fundamental way, they have made a habit of separating fact from fiction, the real from fantasy, substance from symbolism. This kind of thinking does not develop overnight. Whatever the crisis, survivors are already prepared. Why? Because, in some very real ways they have already "been there" before life's inevitable changes occur. They are realists—they already are living in the future as they now know it. Survivors prepare!

For you and me, A.D. 2000 and beyond will not find us parachuting into enemy territory, or on a rail ride into Dachau or Auschwitz. But it will be a fast journey into a world of contradictions and mind-numbing sensory assaults. Decisions that once could be made over months and years are now being forced on us within days and weeks—decisions that will dramatically affect the rest of our lives!

In a cartoon two friends stood on the corner of Fifth and Broadway in New York City, watching two men carrying sandwich signs. One sign said, "The world is about to end." The other, "The world will never end." One bystander said to the other, "One of those men is an optimist, and the other is a pessimist. But I can't tell which is which!"

Those two signs describe most people today. Some look uneasily toward A.D. 2000 and beyond. Others can hardly wait for the "good times to roll." What shall we make of all this?

Let's look, first, at why pessimists and doomsayers are uneasy about the future. What do they think they see? I want to give you a quick overview of seven distinct areas that are causing great concern.

### Religious World

A thousand years ago many Christians believed that the year 1000 meant the end of the world, the apocalypse, the day of God's wrath. Similarly today, anyone who walks through airports has seen serious young people passing out their dreary literature; on our TVs we see and hear wild-eyed evangelists warning that the end is nigh, with a wide assortment of coming terrors.

A misunderstanding of certain prophecies in the book of Revelation (the last book in the New Testament), has permeated recent Hollywood films, many Christian-sponsored films, and certain TV series. *Contact, Armageddon, The Seventh Sign, Asteroid, Deep Impact, Spawn,* as well as Fox's popular *Millennium,* are examples.

Reacting to these misinterpretations of Bible prophecy, groups of people have taken drastic measures. For instance, followers of New Age guru Elizabeth Clare Prophet sold their possessions and moved into Montana bomb shelters, preparatory for Armageddon.

Books such as Hal Lindsey's 1970 best-seller (more than 40 million copies) *The Late Great Planet Earth* and John Walvoord's *Armageddon, Oil and the Middle East Crisis* used current events to explain mysterious biblical images and to fashion intricate end-time scenarios. Their scripts usually involve an event called the rapture, which purportedly will suddenly pull Christians out of the world, leaving nonbelievers to face the great tribulation, a seven-year period ruled by the antichrist. During this time world powers are drawn into a Middle East war, with modern Israel a target of major powers—a war that nearly ends in a nuclear holocaust but is stopped by the return of Jesus.

Those believing in this scenario have identified, in turn, Adolf Hitler, Mikhail Gorbachev, Saddam Hussein, and others as the antichrist of Revelation 13. For them, Cobra helicopters fulfill the biblical symbols of the swarming locusts of Revelation. Some form of this apocalyptic excitement is building for a great number of Christians as the third millennium dawns.

Another feature of this modern misread of Revelation is the focus on credit and debit cards that would contain the "mark of the beast," without which, according to Revelation 13:17, "no man might buy or sell." Proponents believe that the "Beast 666" has been directing the world powers toward a one-world government. At the core of this "universal human control system" (called LUCID) is the high-tech, "smart" ID card called the Universal Biometrics Card. According to certain specialists, this chilling system is supposed to be fully operational in 2000, in time to celebrate the New Age millennium.

This card will place every human being under constant surveillance, just as scientists today monitor birds, fish, whales, and many land animals. All newborns will be entered into the system, and all adults will report to processing centers (perhaps the local post office) and "voluntarily" receive their painless implantation. This embedded "card" or microchip will contain, it is alleged, samples of the individual's DNA genotype, fingerprints, footprints, and iris scans. In other words, no more need for credit cards or personal checks, no more licenses or passports. All this information is fed into a gigantic network called the Universal Computerized Identification Clearinghouse Resource Center, the heart of LUCID. Anyone deemed a "risk to internal security" will be quickly apprehended. Thought crimes will no longer be a matter of science fiction.

According to this scenario, government spin doctors will assure worried citizens that the new system is designed to "protect" them from savage acts of terrorists, that the majority must be protected from "right-wing" conspirators. Anyone who would think differently would be a "dangerous, antigovernment protester." And they no longer could hide, for they could no longer "buy or sell"—they would be "detained," even eliminated!

Other religious thinkers look at the future from a different perspective. They see an unprecedented worldwide ecumenical (unifying) movement among world religions, including but not limited to most Christian denominations.

We have all witnessed an astounding union of once-strong, independent churches. For example, on August 18, 1997, the Evangelical Lutheran Church in America voted to enter into full communion with three other mainstream Protestant denominations—Presbyterian Church (U.S.A.), the Reformed Church in America, and the United Church of Christ (which is the result of an earlier union of the Evangelical and Reformed Church and the Congregational Christian Churches, each being the result of former unions).

These progressive unions are leading inevitably to a virtual mega-Protestant church in the United States. In turn, it will not surprise many to see soon the joint functional union between this mega-Protestant church and the Roman Catholic Church, united on common areas of concern such as social and political action.

What many fear is that this growing momentum for church unity will lead them into a strong political position whereby they can more strongly influence government legislation. Some see in the Christian Coalition and in the deliberate steps to unite Protestants and Catholics in doctrinal unity an increasing capability to enforce definite moral agendas through government action, beginning with such issues as abortion, euthanasia, prayer and Bible study in public schools, and perhaps a combined effort to revive Sunday laws. In other words, many look upon any revival of religious unity and political power as a threat to liberty of conscience for the minority.

### New Age Phenomenon

For many millions, the above scenarios of Armageddon and "smart" ID cards or the chilling, one-church majority focusing on 2000 and beyond are cause for much excitement and unease. But there is another worldwide group, perhaps larger than those already discussed, that puts an altogether different spin on religious expectations focusing on A.D. 2000 and beyond. In recent years a whole new way of looking at the future has emerged for millions of people. Some call this sea change the New Age phenomenon.

The New Age movement appeals to those turned off from organized religion with its hundreds of different quarreling churches and their pitiful misrepresentations of the character of God. Yet the cry for spiritual meaning remains. New Agers refashion biblical terms into a totally different way of thinking about God, Jesus Christ, salvation, and the future life: God becomes universal Breath, human beings are the Breath made flesh, Jesus is humanity's pattern, One who showed us how to fully realize "the divine that is already within us."

Salvation, according to New Agers, is a process of changing our thoughts, without a need for Calvary and the empowerment of the Holy Spirit. Authority regarding truth rests on subjective feeling, not on revelations from a Creator-God. New Agers look for "salvation" from within, not from a personal God; they focus on human potential and the sharing of "felt" experiences with others who have a similar focus. All creation, including humans, is divine and "one," and thus "God" becomes the universal

Energy, the Force. In this oneness, good and evil, even life and death, are the same.

Strange as all this may sound to a biblical Christian, it fits nicely into a post-Christian mind-set in which emphasis on "self-fulfillment" and self-help motivational courses prevails. The problem that faces the New Agers is that they are predisposed to believe anybody who speaks from the "spirit" world, channeling messages from "beyond," appealing for the unity of humanity on issues that are endorsed primarily by feeling, not reason or the authority of Scripture.

The religious overtones and context for the year 2000, contradictory and confusing as they truly are, will drive other issues into a heightened excitement and intensity—all cause for unease.

## Natural Disasters

"Cosmic Storms Coming: Violent outbursts of gas from the surface of the sun could lead to big trouble here on Earth" (*Time,* Sept. 9, 1996). In recent months, headlines like that have become as common as ants at a picnic. Cosmic storms slam communication satellites first, directly affecting the transmission of all sorts of critical data such as credit card transactions, electronic paging, and radio and television transmission. While I was writing this chapter, one of these communication satellites malfunctioned, and more than 90 percent of all pagers in the United States were silent for many days—a terrifying experience for many, and a foretaste of greater problems to come. Space physicists only now are beginning to understand geomagnetic storms, solar events far more awesome than violent sunspots.

In the days before our reliance on super-quick electronic transmission, all this would be nothing to worry about. But today cosmic storms knocking out our satellites may bring about devastating blackouts in space communications. That same *Time* article contained this warning: "The next solar maximum, due sometime around the year 2000, could create worse nightmares" as compared to earlier geomagnetic storms that shut down power grids in North America. For those who know, the next few years could be scary.

### Political Hot Spots

As I write, more than 30 armed conflicts are raging somewhere in the world. The following disputes have the potential to escalate into larger regional wars, possibly the involvement of world powers as they see international trade affected.

- Heading the list would be the conflict in former Yugoslavia, where tens of thousands have been killed and hundreds of thousands made homeless.
- Think of the Chinese-Russian border, especially when (1) the Chinese believe that the present border was the result of unequal treaties and when (2) they see a weakened Russia at a time when China needs underpopulated areas for their expanding population. Or think of China and Taiwan, a ticking time bomb that will not go away.
- Two million Hungarians live in Romania's Transylvania, the largest minority in Europe, and a border war seems imminent.
- India and Pakistan have fought three wars since their independence from Great Britain more than 50

years ago. Their nuclear standoff has alarmed the world.

- The Israel-Arab tension, always on the edge of war, could involve the whole Muslim world. What happens when Israel does not agree to a U.S.-brokered settlement of the West Bank?
- The Korean peninsula has never resolved the war between the North and the South Koreas. With North Korea in a starvation status but also with a million trained soldiers, their leaders may blackmail the South (and the United States) with their unquestioned nuclear capability into some kind of political/social relief.
- Iraq and Syria are furious with Turkey's plan to build a series of hydroelectric dams that will jeopardize the headwaters of the Euphrates and Tigris rivers.
- Turkey and Armenia seem to be inexorably drawn into a showdown over the Azeri-populated enclave of Nakhichevan, an event that would draw NATO Turkey into a war in Russia's oil-rich backyard.
- Russia's unease with the advancing borders of NATO nations that now incorporate former Soviet territories could lead to a military takeover of the Russian government and, with their 800 intercontinental ballistic missiles, put the world on alert.
- Throw in Iraq's Saddam Hussein's remarkable ability to rattle his chains, especially when U.S. forces are occupied in former Yugoslavia, Korea, and elsewhere.
- Look at the complexity existing on the African continent, a land rich with raw materials that all major countries require, now kindled by religious hostilities for which no one has a solution.

## Global Financial Unrest

No one needs to be reminded of the daily headlines that shout recent breakdowns in the financial systems in various regions of the world. The Asian financial situation still remains critical. Asia buys a quarter of U.S. exports; when their purchases fall but their exports, with their lowered prices, to the United States rise, it jeopardizes the sale of U.S. products within this country. All this indicates a troubling storm on the horizon.

One of the hidden realities of the American scene, at a time when we hear that the economy is the best in 30 years, is that personal bankruptcies have never been higher—approaching 1.4 million annually, compared to 300,000 in 1980. In 1990 outstanding bank credit card loans stood at $173 billion; in 1998, $485 billion.[1]

Columnist Robert J. Samuelson wrote that one "would have to go back to the depression of the 1930s to find a global financial crisis—bank failures, mass bankruptcies—that compares with Asia's collapse. By any valuation measures, the stock market is in uncharted territory. The creation of a European currency has no modern parallel; neither does the year 2000 glitch."[2]

## Global Warming

Many reputable scientists ponder the recent signs of global warming. They point to such facts as the twentieth century being the hottest, at least since the fourteenth century, and that February 1998 was a whopping 3.2° F above the average of the past 30 years in the Northern Hemisphere—"by far the most extreme monthly temperature rise ever seen."[3]

Then they point to the polar melt, the 1998 U.S. tornado season (one of the fiercest on record), the documented increase in humidity in the lower atmosphere, the significance in the records of tree rings, ice, and lake sediment layers, all pointing to rising temperatures "attributable to greenhouse gases," and all leading to "significant environmental and economic impacts."[4] Millions of people put the dire warnings of the "greenhouse effect" into their millennial model of frightful happenings in the next few years.

## Space Visitors

In recent years Hollywood has been setting us up with all kinds of movies and TV programs that make space aliens a common topic of conversation. There are *E.T., Close Encounters of the Third Kind, Star Trek, Independence Day, X-Files,* and *Contact* for starters. A group of Taiwanese bought 30 houses in Garland, Texas, in 1998 so that they could wait for God to arrive. They believed that God would send flying saucers to rescue human beings and animals from a coming nuclear war.

Then there was the bizarre mass suicide of the Heaven's Gate cult in the spring of 1997 at their Rancho Santa Fe estate, north of San Diego, California. Many of the 39 members of this "away team" were experts in computer technology. Mixing UFO concepts and New Age theology, the group calmly shed their "containers" (bodies), as they hoped to hitch a ride into the "Next Level" by hooking up to the Hale-Bopp comet, then in spectacular display in the night sky. Some psychologists expect more of the same in the year 2000.

The bottom line: Accustomed to space visitors and intergalactic travel, many people in the next few years will find it only a half step to believing that any report of a space visitor hails the second coming of Jesus Christ. Survivors will keep their heads up, however, and will study the territory ahead in terms of the long view. This long view, which we will discuss later, will keep survivors undistracted as they maneuver through 2000 and beyond.

---

[1] *USA Today,* June 3, 1999.

[2] The Washington *Post,* July 11, 1998.

[3] *US News & World Report,* May 4, 1998.

[4] *Ibid.* Other scientists see in these statistical analyses nothing unusual when they compare the varying trends covering the big picture of thousands of years, especially noting that it was much warmer than today around A.D. 1000.

# Chapter Three

# Survivors Are Realists, Not Mere Optimists

What shall we make of all these worries regarding A.D. 2000 that we looked at in the previous chapter? Depending on a person's point of view, the previous chapter may be either scary or silly. But the pessimists are not all wrong—as we shall see later.

As we noted in chapter 2 regarding those walking billboards, "The World Is *Not* Coming to an End" is the theme song of a worldwide group probably larger than the pessimists. What makes these optimists so happy?

## Remarkable Achievements of the Late-twentieth Century

Problems that seemed formidable only 50 years ago are now forgotten as if they had never existed—or remembered only as relics of long-ago medieval times. Think of what the transistor and microelectronics have done for almost every industry. Or the Salk vaccine (when was the last time we visited a polio victim in the hospital?), CAT and MRI body scanners, Teflon, lasers, organ transplants, polymers, and plastic splices for aneurysms. Or food additives, such as a margarine specially made to reduce cholesterol by preventing the absorption of dietary cholesterol and inhibiting the liver's own production of the heart-clogging fat. According to experts, we can look forward to an increasing cadence of startling and wonderful breakthroughs in the near future.

## Astounding Predictions in Medical Research

Just think of the following promises: a vaccine that prevents cervical cancer, and perhaps many other kinds of cancer as well; underwear that will keep us at exactly the right temperature; certain quadriplegics will regain limited use of their hands (for eating, drinking, shaving, washing, even writing) with the help of an implanted electrical stimulator; baby banks, where prospective parents can browse through profiles of potential sperm and egg donors, customizing their choices to specific physical, ethnic, and occupational characteristics; a single potent vaccine, given at birth, that will prevent tuberculosis, measles, whooping cough, polio, tetanus, and diphtheria, thus saving 8 million children in developing countries annually; drugs that can limit spinal-cord damage when given a few hours after injury, and may be helpful in degenerative ailments such as Alzheimer's disease.

Biotechnology, genetic engineering, and even space-age surgery are no longer the stuff of science fiction. Already we are watching many life-threatening diseases being treated without radical surgery (breakthrough laparoscopy, for instance) or lifelong drug dependency. Physicians have grown new coronary blood vessels by injecting the heart with a bioengineered protein, thus able to skirt blocked arteries.

The amazing speed in deciphering the entire human DNA, or genome, with its 60,000 or so genes, has been far faster and cheaper than first estimates. Genetic engineering pinpoints the faulty genes that cause many of our diseases, inherited and conditioned. These findings not only help physicians diagnose problems even in the womb, they also provide ways by which the mutated gene can be manipulated to offset the potential damage. It has been estimated that half of our drugs in the year 2000 could result from gene therapy.

DNA vaccines will soon be as common as tetanus shots. As I write, researchers are finishing successful experiments with monkeys that promise a DNA vaccine to prevent rabies, which kills 40,000 people annually. DNA vaccines are inexpensive to make and require no refrigeration—a great benefit to developing nations.

Consider the genetically engineered advances made in the cloning of animals. And sooner than we may think, humans.

## Never Out of Touch

Prototypes are now being tested for a pair of everyday prescription eyeglasses that can function as a desktop computer monitor. A cloth keyboard is embroidered on a shirt or jacket, using conductive threads, and a credit-card-sized computer can be housed in the heel of a shoe. Telecommunication will connect this walking computer with the Internet as well as the computerized appliances back home.

### Prospects for Cheaper Energy

The December 1997 issue of *The Trends Journal* predicts that we should be expecting, even before 2000, "the first major public announcements of an energy revolution that promises to free the world of its dependence on fossil fuels." The new energy forms will come out of developments in cold fusion and "zero point energy," the extraction of energy from an apparent vacuum. Many other applications of nonfossil energy, such as wind machines, hydroelectric plants, solar power, hydrogen-driven vehicles, etc., are constantly being improved.

### Agriculture More Than Sufficient

Agricultural researchers are working on resetting the genetic thermostat in many plants whose ideal growing temperature is usually within a very narrow range. The ultimate goal is to create all-weather plants with higher yields, thus adding to the world's supply of food. Some specialists see a giant step forward to harvesting our food through aquaculture, in addition to agriculture. The hunger/starvation problem is not a matter of supply but of distribution, which often is complicated by political forces.

### Population Explosion Diminishes

For decades we have been confronted with a variety of negative consequences of an overpopulated earth, such as resource depletion, ecological damage, and famine. But United Nations reports indicate that the world population will stabilize in 40 years at 7.7 billion—and, even more astonishing, it will then decline!

In the developed nations, the rate has fallen from 2.8 children per woman in the early 1950s to 1.4 today; in the less developed nations, it has fallen from 6 to just under 3. In Europe, not a single country has a fertility rate high enough to maintain its current population. In the United States the fertility rate is barely at replacement level.*

The dire predictions of a world running out of control because of a surplus of people do not seem probable. Yet the implications of a stabilized population level suggest a different set of social problems that most people haven't even had to think about. At least we don't have to expect a worn-out planet, its population suffocating under polluted air, scratching for scraps of food, drowning in its garbage.

### Environmental Experts?

Of course, the world is a safer, more pleasant place to live in today than it was 30 years ago. Lakes and rivers are becoming cleaner, the plight of endangered species is brighter, stricter regulations governing pollution of all kinds are in place. Yet the challenge is ever present.

But many have been the alarms that were wild and unnecessary. The Desert Storm fires did not become "the greatest pollution event in history," as some called it. The Desert Storm eco-hysteria was led by the well-known astronomer Carl Sagan, the clarion voice of the "nuclear winter" frenzy of only a few years ago. He said on *60 Minutes* that the Kuwaiti fires would block out sunlight around the globe, triggering a "petroleum autumn." The group Friends of the Earth predicted that thousands would die.

Although most scientists believe that these doom-and-gloomers are wrong, they aren't the ones who get interviews on TV or appointments to speak at college campuses. It is the false predictions that are applauded, so long as they are scary enough.

Paul Ehrlich, guru of environmentalism, predicted in his 1968 book, *The Population Bomb,* that there would be food riots in the United States by 1977, and that India's food production would decline. But India's food production has doubled since 1968. He also predicted that the world was running out of natural resources such as grain, oil, timber, coal, and metals. The low prices for these commodities in 1998 indicate that they are plentiful.

Human beings love calamities; they crave stimulation. Check the latest newspaper or TV news. It seems that gullibility is a perennial disease, especially during times of uncertainty such as we are facing as we count down to 2000.

### What Shall We Make of All This Optimism?

The list of vast changes to come is endless. What we do know is that the future will be incredibly creative, full of timesaving, space-saving ingenuities. It could be a world free from disease (except for lifestyle diseases such as cardiovascular problems, most diabetes, high blood pressure, etc.), and full of instant entertainment at the click of a remote control.

Referring once again to the cartoon of the pessimists and the optimists, however, the survivor will recognize that both are wrong. The pessimists should be realistic—the world will not end in either a whimper or a bang. World nuclear powers will not incinerate the earth; we will not drown or be suffocated in our own garbage, nor shrivel up in mass starvation.

But the optimists are also wrong—the future is not in the hands of ingenious men and women who, till now, have always come up with the necessary solutions to whatever problem. Technology will not cure, for example, the self-interest of relatives or neighbors, or nations, as they grab for what they have not earned, trampling others in their pursuit. Technology may recycle used glass and metals but not the moral garbage that mocks the rising standards of living everywhere on this planet.

Technology will not eliminate deceit and spinmeisters who make a career out of repackaging morally deficient leaders. Technology will not be able to produce trust and fairness—regardless of Hollywood's ability to substitute style for substance.

What indeed could be more suffocating than a disease-cured world, filled with homes with the latest computerized labor-saving devices, and guaranteeing adequate food for every man, woman, and child (all very probable expectations)—if that world wallows in its material comforts and sensual excesses but scorns the time-honored values of respect for property rights, responsibility, honesty, purity and fidelity in marriage, and all other relationships?

Survivors know their territory. They are realists.

They are not suckered by the zeal of the optimist or the fears of the pessimist. They prepare for the future with their eyes wide open to the real world, to those things that matter most. Survivors are prepared! They will be calm, alert, responsible parents, coworkers, and community leaders in 2000 and beyond. They focus on the long view.

---

*Charles Krauthammer, in Dallas *Morning News,* July 19, 1998.

*Chapter Four*

# Survivors Think Preparedness

All of us have discovered that life is full of surprises. For most people, the future does not unfold as planned. Frightful accidents often change a person's life forever. Financial security may vanish like the morning fog, forcing us to rethink our plans about college, or to make room in our homes for parents who no longer are capable of caring for themselves. Readers can add their own stories of surprises and changed plans.

If anyone in the Bible was a survivor, it surely was the prophet Jeremiah. Jeremiah had many difficult experiences that were not of his making. In Jeremiah 12 the prophet bared his soul with God. He wondered, as many of us have done on occasion, why it seems that the wicked prosper, and why those who deal treacherously seem so happy.

God answered Jeremiah with words that we need to hear often. Survivors have heeded these words for many centuries: "If you have run with the footmen, and they have wearied you, then how can you contend with horses? And if in the land of peace, in which you trusted, they wearied you, then how will you do in the floodplain of the Jordan?" (Jer. 12:5, NKJV).

Survivors prepare to run with the horses. In times of peace they have been preparing for flood times, not in panic but with a steady, heads-up lifestyle. Survivors think long-term when others think in terms of instant gratification. I can guarantee that someday in your life, maybe sooner than later, the Jordan will swell, the easy paths will suddenly become treacherous with foes unseen, the wind will become brisk, the hill steeper. Past history, even parents and teachers, will not provide all the answers. What then?

A young man who worked for Lord Joseph Duveen suggests an answer. Duveen headed up an American art firm that bore his name. In 1915, during World War I, he planned to send one of his experts to England to examine some ancient pottery. After he booked passage on the *Lusitania* for this specialist, the German Embassy issued a warning that the liner might be torpedoed. Wanting to call off the trip, Duveen told his employee that he couldn't take the risk of him being killed.

"'Don't worry,' the young man replied. 'I'm a strong swimmer, and when I read what was happening in the North Atlantic, I began hardening myself by spending time every day in a tub of ice water. At first I could stand it only a few minutes, but this morning I stayed in that tub nearly two hours.'

"Naturally, Duveen laughed. It sounded preposterous. But his expert sailed; the *Lusitania* was torpedoed. The young man was rescued after nearly five hours in the chilly ocean, still in excellent condition."*

As we said in the previous chapter, survivors know their territory. They are realists. They prepare for the future while all is calm. Duveen's young expert was a survivor. He knew well what could happen in the North Atlantic. And he knew what it would take to survive. He was not surprised by the future.

### Five Areas That Identify Survivors

We need to make an inventory today of our preparation for whatever surprise or crisis may be around the next turn in the road. I can think of five areas that need special attention while we still have time and opportunity to prepare for the unknown—physical stamina, economic independence, mental vigor and habit patterns, moral muscle, and clarity of purpose. Swimming in the North Atlantic may not require economic security, but it surely calls for physical, mental, and moral preparation for the unknown. Survivors think like survivors long before the test comes.

I know that for some the pages ahead may be different from anything you have ever read. But make no mistake, strengthening and maintaining physical health is not one of life's options. That is, if you want to think like, and be, a survivor. Each page will provide a fresh look at some changes you may want to make immediately. But these changes can become such a natural part of your life you'll wonder how you ever got along without them.

Every time you face a suggestion, don't ask, Why do I have to do that? Ask, Why not? The future will not be kind to the unprepared. But the rewards of preparation are great. You are about to discover a lifestyle program in which survival is not a morbid obsession. Thinking like a survivor was not a grim, dreary preparation for the young man who survived the North Atlantic.

I am not a pessimist who sees only trouble ahead. Neither am I a romantic idealist who ignores those same problems. I determine to be a realist, aware of the potholes in the road of life but absolutely committed to working my way around, maybe even through, them. I enjoy life's white-water rapids, building the dream house and landscaping it as time permits, embracing our six children with all their hopes and dreams and disappointments, and above all else, responding professionally to whatever the next assignment may be.

But all of this could vanish quickly if I am overmedicated, physically drained, and emotionally exhausted. If I ignore the simple laws of health, if I forget how to handle stress, if I lose sight of the big picture and lose the ability to endure under tough times, all my ability to be useful stops. I even become a burden to others.

So for my sake and yours, let's have a commonsense understanding of what it means to be healthy and strong. In the next chapter we will note how survivors look at the first, unavoidable step in preparing for the future. Money in the bank cannot substitute for this first step. Neither can a great job or a prize spouse. Nor can one's genetic code make up the difference. I am talking about your health.

Tomorrow is not for the weak! Those who truly survive in 2000 and beyond are not prophets, but they prepare as if they did know the future! They know that the prepared begin with what they control, their health.

---

*Vernon C. Grounds, "Getting Into Shape Spiritually," *Christianity Today,* Feb. 2, 1979.

# Chapter Five

# Survivors Think Wellness

How should survivors think about their physical well-being? The question is fundamental, not only to avoid the high costs of health care, but also to find the stamina for survival. Further, the question is not academic.

Close to a million times a year in the United States, someone has a heart attack. The first attack is often that person's last. More than 53 percent of all deaths (in the U.S.) are the result of coronary heart disease and stroke. Most of these horrible and sudden events are preventable. A survivor asks, How?

Or, instead of a sudden surprise such as a heart attack, there is that slow, lingering death from cancer, a word that freezes on one's tongue. In the United States alone, it kills annually some 500,000 people. And it costs more than $30 billion annually. The survivor asks, How can I prevent cancer?

These two diseases alone account for three fourths of all deaths in the United States. That is 1,450,000 people—more Americans *each year* than were killed in every war from the American Revolution to Vietnam put together!

But there is good news. *We already know how to cut the risk of death from heart attack by at least 50 percent!* Further, medical research indicates that the overall risk of death from cancer could be cut 80 percent simply by using some commonsense ideas we already know.

The fascinating side of these statistics is that by making certain commonsense ideas a daily habit, we would be putting money in the bank as well as preserving health. No longer would we be paying big money for drugs to deal with cardiovascular problems or cancer treatment. No longer would we be buying certain foods that cost more than the commonsense diet that promises a high degree of freedom from cancer and heart attacks.

So let's begin. How does the survivor rise above cancer, cardiovascular disease, high blood pressure, diabetes, and other diseases?

### Seven Basic Health Laws

Dr. Lester Breslow, dean of the School of Public Health at the University of California, Los Angeles, with fellow researchers in the Human Population Laboratory of the California State Department of Public Health, began a study of 7,000 adult residents of Alameda County, California, in 1965. Their studies led to the conclusion that *good health habits, rather than a person's initial health status,* were responsible for a remarkable extension of life expectancy.

Through the years that followed, Dr. Breslow has checked and rechecked his statistics, and the results are always the same. He believes that the future of medicine lies in the prevention of disease, not just in its treatment.[1]

What are his conclusions that startled the scientific community? Simply, that Americans could add *11 extra years* to their lives by following *seven commonsense health habits*. Here are Dr. Breslow's seven rules:

- Don't smoke.
- Use little or no alcohol.
- Start the day with a good breakfast.
- Avoid eating between meals.
- Sleep seven to eight hours each night.
- Engage in frequent, regular exercise.
- Maintain ideal weight.

Perhaps you were expecting something more exotic or some magic bullets. Perhaps these seven habits seem too simple to promise 11 extra years.

### Looking at the Data

Let's look at Dr. Breslow's data. For nine years they studied their population group, correlating health habits with death rates. Get this: If an American man routinely broke *just one* of these seven rules—avoid eating between meals, for example—his survival probability after just nine years dropped by 40 percent!

After nine years a smoker's risk of dying increased by almost 70 percent. Heavy drinkers increased their risk by 36 to 46 percent.

The stunning observation is this: None of these seven habits for greater longevity require a costly investment in drug therapy! None of these seven habits add one cent to the family budget! To the contrary, all of these seven habits are destined to save money that could be spent more profitably, more enjoyably.

Let's take a closer look at Breslow's seven habits.

**1. For Those Who Smoke—**

Nonsmokers can enjoy a risk factor of 80 percent less than that of their smoking friends. Consider also the other advantages: a much lower risk of death from mouth, throat, and bladder cancers; a greatly reduced danger of getting the terrible disability called emphysema, in which every breath becomes hard work, requiring eventually a breathing machine connected to you for the rest of your shortened, miserable life. Further, the nonsmoker will enjoy much better physical endurance and night vision, lowered risk of heart disease, and avoidance of Raynaud's disease (fingertips become blue and painful).

We know that for many, trying to stop smoking has not been easy. In fact, it may be the hardest challenge some people face. I have some suggestions for you. You will be glad to know that much lung damage can be reversed within a few years after cessation of smoking.

Although going cold turkey is possible for some, most smokers need help when they choose to stop. Many commercial programs are available, some of them expensive. Perhaps the most effective aid is called Zyban; its value in breaking the smoking habit was discovered by Dr. Linda Ferry, chief of the Preventive Medicine Section at the Jerry L. Pettis Veteran Affairs Medical Center in Loma Linda, California. This medication, known also as bupropion, is the first FDA-approved, nonaddicting, nonnicotine prescription that changes the neurochemistry in the smoker's brain. It decreases the problems of nicotine dependency and withdrawal. C. Everett Koop, M.D., said that Dr. Ferry's research has given nicotine addicts "the best assurance they have ever had that they can quit smoking."

Through the years programs such as the Five-Day Plan to Stop Smoking and the Breathe-Free Plan have been offered by the Seventh-day Adventist Church in hundreds of communities. Hundreds of thousands of serious smokers have stopped smoking through these programs.

Here are some of the tips that former smokers have used:

- Believe you can stop, even as more than 30,000,000 have before you. All survivors have learned the power of saying "I choose . . ." whatever the goal may be. "I choose not to smoke" is the first and most important step on the road to success.
- Use plenty of water. None of us drink enough, at best. But a smoker's body is permeated with nicotine, which must be flushed out as soon as possible. Drink at least 8 to 10 glasses daily between meals, not with your meals. Many have found that two glasses of warm water immediately after rising in the morning jump-starts the day. The best way is to record your glasses each day, because memories get fuzzy. Don't think that this step is unimportant. Besides, it costs nothing. In fact, get into the habit, because eight glasses of water daily is part of a healthy survivor's lifestyle.

But you need plenty of water outside your body

as well. You can't overdo a relaxing bath or shower. Use a sauna or a hot tub as often as possible. You will need every advantage to relieve the distressing symptoms of nicotine withdrawal. Besides, it is hard to smoke in the shower. Get into the survivor's habit of starting off with a hot shower, then a cold shower for maybe a minute. Perhaps you will think at first that a survival attitude is not worth it, but don't give up—that cold water every day will become one of your strongest allies in preparing you for the future. For instance, hot and cold showers do much to improve your immune system. Go through several cycles, especially during the nicotine withdrawal period. Blood vessels that nicotine have made sluggish need to be jump-started into a happier tomorrow.

• Drinking coffee makes the effort to stop smoking much more difficult. Coffee has been called the "bad-habit glue." Think about it! When you sit down to a cup of coffee, what do you reach for next? Right, a cigarette! If you must reach into that shirt pocket or purse, pick up some sugarless gum. For the same reason, this is a good time to avoid beer, wine, or hard liquor. Nothing must be done to weaken or deaden your willpower.

• Pamper yourself, especially during this stressful week—get plenty of sleep. Make a point of getting at least eight hours' sleep each night. Again, your willpower needs the help of extra sleep.

• After meals, leave the table immediately. If you sit around, the old habit of reaching for a cigarette will bite you. Head for a brisk walk where you will not find the smell of cigarettes that reminds you of the "pleasant" sensation you have associated with cigarettes. If you could have your curtains, drapes, and carpets cleaned during the week, you will be removing one more subtle reminder of your former "enjoyment" with smoking.

• Do anything to keep your mind off yourself. Play golf or tennis. Increase your jogging or walking—anything outside in the fresh air. Breathe deeply. Your body always needs oxygen, and exercise is the greatest contributor.

• Avoid heavily spiced foods, fried food, and rich desserts. You ask, What does all this have to do with quitting smoking? Often unaware, smokers have deadened taste buds, forcing them to use more and more seasonings and "tastier" food, just to enjoy their food. In fact, when you stop smoking, taste buds will return to normal, and you won't need highly spiced or rich foods.

• Eat those foods that the American Cancer Society recommends: fresh fruit, vegetables, wholesome grains. Cut down on your use of salt. With less salt your weight may be easier to control, and your blood pressure surely will be. You may also need some extra B vitamins as your body strives to flush out nicotine poison.

• You should know that the powerful forces of the Almighty are waiting for your call. This promise has helped millions to discard tobacco, "I can do all things through Christ who strengthens me" (Phil. 4:13, NKJV).[2]

**2. Something Better Than Alcohol**

Breslow's data simply reinforced what reasonable

people have observed for millennia. He found that those who regularly had four or more alcoholic drinks at a time suffered a 36 percent increase in the risk of death over the nine-year period of his first study. Alcohol is associated with head and neck cancers, in addition to the liver and pancreas. When combined with smoking, alcohol increases the risk of oral cancer dramatically. Half of our traffic accidents are caused by alcohol consumption. Think of the enormous costs to the family and nation.

**3. A Heart-healthy Breakfast**

Something strange has happened to America and many other countries during the past 100 years. Breakfast used to be a big meal, but not today for most families. Why? Because of a heavy, perhaps late, dinner after a lengthy evening of TV watching, our body tries long into the night to digest the meal. At breakfasttime the next day the body simply is not ready for another meal. So before they dash out the front door, most people, if lucky, grab a glass of orange juice and a doughnut. Or, even more likely, it is a cup or two of coffee and then out the door.

Later in the morning the body cries for a pickup because the drug stimulant in the coffee has worn off. So what's next, about 10:00 a.m.? The snack bar, another doughnut, more coffee, or a caffeinated drink with more empty calories—and the body gets another fake pickup. At noon junk food full of fat at a fast-food stop. We may be used to this program, but the body is ready to cry out for help. Nerves are jangling, irritation with others is easily tripped, and feelings of being mistreated or ignored rise to the surface—all because of a lack of essential vitamins and minerals that was not eaten in a well-balanced breakfast.

What happens when the weary and drained hit the late afternoon traffic? Impatience, perhaps road rage! We feel sorry for ourselves, and our evening meal becomes the gratification for a hard day's work or study. "We deserve it," we tell ourselves, and seek a meal that first must please the taste buds (read full of fat). Understandably tired from a day of stress and now laden with a heavy meal, we hardly entertain the thought of exercise; it is easily overcome with the newspaper in one hand and the TV clicker in the other. Then to bed, only to start the miserable routine all over again.

What's wrong here? No adequate breakfast! No morning meal to break-the-fast of the night, which should have been preceded by a light supper, if any. Breslow's data cries out for a healthful breakfast. Why? With a good breakfast the whole day becomes manageable; the body is now working for you and not controlling your moods or time schedule. Remember, *Breslow's irrefutable research points out that the middle-age American male who eats a great breakfast enjoys a 40 percent higher survival rate than his neighbor who grabs the doughnut and coffee, or less.*

After a hearty breakfast, midmorning snacktime becomes an opportunity to drink more water and to get some exercise, preferably outdoors—not a time to add empty calories and more dangerous fats and sugars to the only body you have. Breslow pointed out that between-meal snacks caused a 20 percent mortality increase! Remember, survivors think long-term; they realize that their first line of defense is their own health.

What might an adequate breakfast be? Let your mouth water over an orange and a banana alongside your bowl of sugar-free whole-grain cereal. Perhaps date bits and raisins liberally sprinkled in the cereal. Try skim milk on your cereal, or some milk substitute. (There are plenty out there.) Using grape juice, I make my granola into a dessert. Some make their breakfast their largest meal of the day, with vegetables, salads, legumes, etc.—the whole works.

The point is to make breakfast a hearty mix of vitamins and minerals that will fuel your body for the day ahead, without the false pickup and subsequent damage of coffee and sugary pastries.

What about that evening meal that should set us up for a great sleep and prepare us for that scrumptious breakfast? You have already had your daily supply of energy-producing food. Your brain is not foggy. If you need an evening meal, make it light and easily digestible, such as fresh fruit. You will not feel like crashing on the TV couch. You will have time for the family, for that book that you wanted to read, for working on a hobby, and especially for that daily 30-minute walk. All this because of a good breakfast!

### 4. Those Snacks

What are most snacks made of? They are usually high in salt, sugar, and saturated fat, which only adds to the cholesterol or diabetic problem of even young people these days, never mind their parents. Make a habit of reading the nutrition labels and, when possible, turn away from anything that lists "hydrogenated fat" or "saturated fat" as an ingredient.

Besides the "empty calories" (calories with diminished nutritional value) and dangerous food combinations contained in most items eaten between meals, the increasing damage to our digestive tract that rarely gets a time to relax will soon show up in medical problems. Further, empty calories play games with us at the proper mealtime; we don't feel hungry enough to eat the foods loaded with nourishment and fiber that our bodies need for maximum health. Survivors think about such things.

No wonder men who regularly ate between meals suffered a 20 percent mortality increase.

### 5. Don't Feel Guilty About Rest

In Dr. Breslow's study, men who regularly slept less than six hours a night had a 36 percent greater death rate than men who slept seven to eight hours.

Sleep is part of our life cycle, and what we do during the day directly affects our sleep pattern. Heavy suppers and lack of exercise cause restless sleep! Exercise is the cheapest sleeping pill.

What shall we say about worry and anxiety? We all have discovered that no problem looks as bad in daylight as it does at 3:00 a.m. Survivors need their sleep as part of their preparation for whatever surprise comes down the road. If you have faith in God and know through experience the power of biblical promises, you already have the secret of getting through those nights that seem to explode with the problems of the day. If you don't have this trusting relationship with your Best Friend, let's see if we can work this out before you finish this book. The future will be a terribly lonely and scary place for those who do not have a strong grip on the everlasting arm of your Best Friend.

### 6. Regular Exercise

In studying the statistics of the past 10 years, one of the most gratifying things to note is that the number of heart attacks nationally has peaked and is actually decreasing! Researchers agree that the tremendous emphasis in the mass media on the need for exercise is, to a large extent, responsible for this good trend. Also, it seems the general public is far more aware of other means of reducing heart-related problems, such as avoiding saturated fat, not smoking, and better blood-pressure control. For example, a healthy diet may not be enough to ward off heart disease. Studies of those at risk indicate that LDL, or "bad" cholesterol, levels fell 13 percent in men and 9 percent in women who combined a low-fat diet with exercise; for those who changed only their diet, the drop was only half of those percentages.[3]

Exercise, along with a healthy diet, directly affects not only our general well-being but also the effects of diabetes, angina, and high-blood pressure. At the Newstart Lifestyle Center, a component of Weimar Institute in Weimar, California, I observed many hundreds of severe diabetic guests, men and women of all ages. They came in wheelchairs or struggling with their walkers or canes. When they left the institute most of them were walking two to four miles daily—

and on reduced medication or none at all! Were they happy? They went home motivated to keep up with their walking program and a healthy diet.

Yes, I said "walking." Most everybody can walk, even arthritic sufferers. Walking avoids some of the long-range problems of jogging. To get real value, we should walk at least 20 minutes without stopping. Research has indicated that it takes at least that long for exercise to benefit the heart and lungs.

Don't measure yourself against someone else. Just start walking, even if slowly. You will find that in a few days you will be walking for more than 20 minutes, always increasing your distance. The object is to get your pulse rate up to a target level, which is computed in a simple way to ensure your safety. Take the number 200 and subtract from that number your age. To be extra safe, knock off another 10 percent from that figure. That is your target pulse rate (beats per minute). Each time you exercise, you should try to get your pulse rate up to (but not over) that number.

How much will walking cost you? Probably an extra pair of good walking shoes annually and a half hour a day. Dividends? Less medicine, if any, great sleep, and a positive look into the future.

In Breslow's study, men who never exercised had 274 percent greater risk of death within the nine years of his study than did the men who exercised briskly!

### 7. Be Good to Yourself—Find Your Ideal Weight

The last of Breslow's seven basic health principles is not the least. A weight-management program consists of (1) eating a good breakfast; (2) skipping the snacks; (3) skipping the empty and refined calories; (4) reducing the intake of animal products; (5) eating a light supper, or none at all; and (6) brisk exercise, at least 30 minutes or more daily. That's it!

How does one eliminate empty and refined calories? Pounds come off quickly and stay off when one eats a nutritious diet without visible fats and refined sugar. Pounds stay off when one eats unrefined products such as whole-grain breads, brown rice, and whole-grain cereals. Watch out for the grocery shelves loaded with so-called healthy cereals, even granola. In the list of ingredients, you will find a heavy sugar content, some as high as 60 percent!

Visible fats include shortening, most salad oils, and most margarines. Check the labels for hydrogenated ingredients. Cook your favorite foods in a teflon-lined fry pan without oil. Use fewer greasy spreads on your bread.

Greatly reducing the use of refined sugar seems so obvious. That includes sweet rolls and doughnuts for breakfast, ice cream, pies, and cakes for desserts. We are not necessarily talking about a total elimination of desserts for everybody. But I am talking to those who sincerely want to manage their weight until it hovers at the ideal.

How much is too much sugar? One regular-size cola drink has about six teaspoons of sugar. Twelve teaspoons of sugar reduce disease resistance by 60 percent. Twenty-four teaspoons virtually destroy one's ability to fight disease. Yet an average banana split carries 25 teaspoons of sugar!

To make all this even more graphic, when we combine sugar with fat (such as in ice cream) we not only pull down the fences in our immune system but introduce the raw materials that contribute to heart disease. Sugar also robs the system of vitamins essential for healthy nerve and brain function. Of course, we like something sweet. Try naturally sweet foods such as fruit.

In addition, weight management rules out alcohol drinking. Not only is alcohol high in empty calories; it also depresses your willpower—and who needs willpower more than one working with weight management!

One more definite help in reducing weight is to reduce or eliminate entirely the use of animal products.

## What's Wrong With Animal Products?

Saturated fats, such as those in animal products, cause the body to produce excess cholesterol, which has much to do with atherosclerosis, the blocking of arteries. Further, meat has none of the plant fiber necessary for healthy digestion and elimination. Cholesterol, which might have been carried off by fiber, lingers longer in the stomach and thus is more easily reabsorbed into the bloodstream. Much research indicates that animal products have a direct connection to various cancers, such as colon cancer. Colon cancer kills about 50,000 Americans annually—nearly as many deaths as American deaths during nine years of war in Vietnam!

Let's review Breslow's research, statistics that continue to affirm his first study in 1965. At the end of his nine-year study, the comparison of mortality rates was stunning. Those who observed all seven rules had only a 5.2 percent chance of dying within the nine-year period of the study. Those who followed six of the rules had more than twice the mortality rate of those who practiced the seven! And those who observed three or fewer had a 20 percent chance of dying within the nine-year period. In other words, when it comes to health, everything is connected to everything else.

*Caution: We don't want any readers to give up because they are not following all seven at the moment. There is value in doing just one of the seven! The point is, start where you are and plug in one rule after another. You will soon begin to see the benefits of each one of the rules.*

Survivors are realists, and they build on common sense. That is why they will survive with a smile in 2000 and beyond.

---

[1] Among numerous references to the Breslow studies, the reader will enjoy reading an article by Breslow and James E. Enstrom, entitled "Persistence of Health Habits and Their Relationship to Mortality," *Preventive Medicine* 9 (1980): 469-483.

[2] The American Cancer Society lists the following benefits of quitting smoking:

**Within 20 Minutes**

- Blood pressure drops to normal.
- Pulse rate drops to normal.
- Body temperature of hands and feet increases to normal.

**Within 8 Hours**

- Carbon monoxide level in blood drops to normal.
- Oxygen level in blood increases to normal.

**Within 24 Hours**

- Chance of heart attack decreases.

**Within 48 Hours**

- Nerve endings start regrowing.
- Ability to smell and taste is enhanced.

**Within 2 Weeks to 3 Months**

- Circulation improves.
- Walking becomes easier.
- Lung function increases up to 30 percent

**Within 1 to 9 Months**

- Coughing, sinus congestion, fatigue, shortness of breath decrease.
- Cilia regrow in lungs, reducing infection.
- Body's overall energy increases.

**Within 1 Year**

- Excess risk of coronary heart disease is cut by half.

**Within 5 Years**

- Lung cancer death rate for average former smoker decreases by almost half.
- Stroke risk is reduced to that of a nonsmoker 5-15 years after quitting.
- Risk of cancer of mouth, throat, and esophagus is half that of smokers.

**Within 10 Years**

- Lung cancer death rate similar to that of nonsmokers.
- Precancerous cells are replaced.
- Risk of cancer of the mouth, throat, esophagus, bladder, kidney, and pancreas decreases.

**Within 15 Years**

- Risk of coronary heart disease is that of nonsmokers.

(Cited in *The World Almanac,* 1997 [Mahwah, N.J.: World Almanac Books, 1996], p. 163.)

[3] *Time,* July 13, 1998.

Chapter Six

# Survivors Use Stress Creatively

No one can avoid stress. Even happy, successful people face tension and pressures, such as when the word processor suddenly goes blank and a whole chapter is lost! In fact, those who choose to live honorably and unselfishly may face stressful circumstances that others are never bothered with. In other words, no one is immune; everyone needs to learn how to cope with stress. And every stressful situation, good or bad, causes biochemical reactions in our bodies—physically, mentally, and emotionally.

But what exactly is stress? Stress is easier to describe than to define. We have all experienced the upset stomach, the goose pimples, the headache, the rapid pulse. Adrenaline flows, digestion stops, as the body gears up to fight or flee—like what happens to a cat when it is cornered by a dog.

Dr. Hans Selye, probably the foremost authority on stress, defines it as what happens to the body after any kind of stimulation or demand, whether a good or bad experience. Medical research indicates that 80 percent or more of our common physical problems, such as colitis, constipation, diarrhea, hemorrhoids, back pains, insomnia, fatigue, high blood pressure, and the common cold, begin as emotional reactions to life's stressors. Worse, stress can be as harmful as bad cholesterol, causing growth of artery plaques and eventually heart attacks.

### How Do Survivors Cope?

How do healthy survivors cope with stress? First, they have learned to recognize the difference between short-term and long-term stress. Short-term stress or anxiety for some people would include a visit to the dentist, or a having to make a speech, or forgetting someone's name when trying to introduce them. Long-term stress or anxiety would include illness, family problems, or a job that is boring or unpleasant. We call these long-term tensions "chronic stress."

When we find ourselves saying "When will it ever end?" or "It will always be this way—there's no hope for anything different!"—then we know we are setting ourselves up to the inevitable consequences of chronic stress. Those who feel "locked-in" to negative circumstances often compensate with typical responses such as overeating, alcoholic binges, credit-card splurges, and extramarital affairs.

Often no solution seems on the horizon for long-range stress. But survivors stand back and look at the inevitable life-threatening consequences staring them in the face. They realize that they may not be able to change these circumstances, however they have decided that those circumstances will not control them.

They make a habit of saying to themselves: "I will pay attention to my health." "I will not let someone else ruin me." "I will choose to take a walk rather than retaliate." "I will not tackle all my responsibilities at once; I will take them one at a time."

The next lesson survivors learn as they begin to take charge of life's circumstances (reducing stress) is to remember that they are largely what they eat. They begin with what they truly can control—their own health. In addition to eating heart-healthy meals, they take the advice of nutrition specialists who recommend a good B-complex vitamin after meals, with an increased intake of calcium and magnesium.

Exercise becomes a daily companion, not only to keep the heart and circulatory system in premium shape, but also to enjoy the release of endorphins, the mood-elevating chemicals in the brain. The endorphin hormone is one of God's gifts to humanity. It works like morphine but without that drug's side effects.

### Warning Signs

What are some of the warning signs of problem anxiety or chronic stress?

• Normal functions are impaired. Assignments normally done with relative ease now become burdensome, boring, or "too much." We are more easily distracted, and we find ourselves reviewing items over and over again. Life is becoming less organized, perhaps chaotic.

• We resort to verbal hostility, even physical attacks, that surprise us as well as others. Feeling overwhelmed, perhaps even incompetent, may cause us to yell at others, slam doors, make threats, and otherwise lose control.

• New patterns develop, such as compulsive perfectionism, hoarding, inordinate list-making, or talking incessantly. Often a person may repeatedly ask for reassurance from others, either in the home or at work.

• Withdrawal from normal activities. We feel inadequate or uncomfortable about sharing our feelings. We would rather avoid people and confrontation, even refuse invitations for social affairs and the attempts of others to be friendly.

• Physical signs would include a feeling of being smothered, shortness of breath, difficulty in swallowing, sweating, chest pain, nausea, rapid heart beat, fear of dying or of going crazy.

## First Step in Managing Stress

Being a realist, the survivor is aware that stress and anxiety can be:

• A positive force in one's life. The biochemical reactions noted above are telling us that something is wrong, that change is needed, that we need to slow down and examine the cause of our fears. The first step in anxiety management, or coping with stress, is to determine how all these signals are your friends. Survivors realize that even normally happy people feel anxious from time to time. But survivors learn how to control their stressors, rather than having them control the survivor!

• A sign thát professional intervention may be indicated. Of course, this is a difficult decision because the line between normal anxiety and chronic anxiety is not always clear. Often one of the symptoms of chronic stress/anxiety is that the sufferer withdraws from others, thus aggravating the problem. If ever one needs to talk with a wise, sympathetic friend, layperson, or professional, it is now.

### Tips on Preventing Normal Stress From Becoming Distress

Survivors learn how to keep normal anxiety/stress from becoming distress or chronic anxiety. Here are some tips:

- Whenever possible, set aside difficult problems for a specific length of time. Far from denying their existence, this ability to turn to another focus entirely different from the immediate stressor provides time to get perspective. For example, instead of bringing work home from the office, take the family out for the evening or weekend. Visit a museum or a historical site, or perhaps go for a swim in the lake or ocean. Work on a hobby or take a long walk.
- Return to basics in the daily schedule. Rise earlier in the morning and provide time for daily devotional reading and prayer; eat the hearty breakfast we recommend so often. Make your list for the day and do the most difficult tasks first. Separate what can wait and what you have to do now.
- During the daily or weekly schedule, change environment from time to time. Take vigorous walks, an extra shower. Make deliberate, special calls to someone who needs encouragement.
- Shut up! Stop interrupting and arguing. Maybe

the other person is right. In most everyday circumstances, even if the other person is wrong, so what?

• View problems as challenges. Try to solve them, one by one.

• Whenever possible, develop a special confidante, someone who has proved his or her trustworthiness, someone you admire and who shares common ideals.

• Focus on tested models in your profession or in your role as a parent. For me, above all others, that model is Jesus Christ, who has shown us all how to endure tough times, loneliness, and unfair accusations.

• Caution: Even the best of these pointers could become only Band-aids at best if we do not yield to our best Friend, the Creator of the universe, as naturally as the flower bends to the sun, as enthusiastically as our grandchildren jump into our backyard pool. Yielding to Him does not mean avoidance of reality. Rather, yielding to His will means that we are putting ourselves into a relationship in which He can return to us His creative power and peace. More about this later.

## Personality Types A and B

One of the more interesting concepts that have emerged in the past 25 years focuses on personality profiles and their connection with chronic anxiety problems and heart failure. After studying 3,000 people for approximately 15 years, Drs. Friedman and Rosenman, two San Francisco heart specialists, concluded that most people prone to heart failure possess a common personality profile they called Type A. Those less prone were called Type B.

| *Type A Characteristics* | *Type B Characteristics* |
| --- | --- |
| Excessive ambition | Appear easygoing, relaxed |
| Achievement-oriented | Pleasure-oriented |
| Marked impatience | Not time-oriented |
| Dissatisfaction with self | Satisfaction with self |

Obviously, most people are a blend of both types in varying degrees. But in general, Type A people tend not to be satisfied with the present, never really sure who they are today, out to prove something or become someone not yet attained, and in a hurry to do it. Type B people, in general, are less competitive, more accepting of life's circumstances, content with who they are regardless of their state of goodness or apathy. Rarely is any-one a pure A or B; rather, they are more likely either AB or BA.

## The Third Choice, Type C

So I have coined (as far as I know!) the term "Type C." Dr. Hans Selye was asked, "If you had to give one piece of advice to people about stress, what would you say to them?" His answer: "I would offer the wisdom of the Bible, translated into terms a scientist can easily accept today: 'Earn thy neighbor's love.'"*

Selye's wisdom is the flip side of Christ's response to the question "Which is the great commandment in the law?" Jesus said, "You shall love the Lord your God with all your heart, and with all your soul, and with all your mind. This is the great and first commandment. And a second is like it, You shall love your neighbor as yourself" (Matt. 22:36-39, RSV).

Christ's response is more than a theological statement; it is the great prescription from the Great Physician for managing stress. Both Type A and Type B need Selye's wisdom and Christ's prescription. More than Type A's self-actualization, more than Type B's self-satisfaction, Type C individuals simultaneously join self-commitment with self-denial to a Person higher than themselves.

Thus, Type C personalities are:

- Committed to personal relationships, with both God and their fellowmen.
- Service-oriented in the pursuit of excellence, whatever the lifework.
- Open to unfolding truth—firm on conviction, open to the new.
- Able to forgo self-interest for the sake of others.
- Focused on being responsible without pressing constantly to be No. 1.

Type C's best model is Jesus Christ. It is the way of love. Type C personalities discover that the highest ideal in life is not to live up to their ego ideal, or even constantly attempting to live up to their own Christian commitments by sheer willpower alone. (That is really stressful!) On the contrary, the more they commit to a personal relationship with God and unselfish love, the more they truly accomplish, the more they are wanted, and the more liberated they are from stressful living.

Even survivors carry baggage from the past. But survivors have learned to reverse these self-condemnations of a chronic worrier. These feelings, if believed, are the land mines that wound, even destroy, the individual.

How do survivors do it? They have listened to the words of Jesus that tell them very clearly that, with His help, *we don't have to be what we are, we don't have to get what we may deserve, and each person is very important and worth a lot.* God tells us plainly that we are not orphans and thus alone in this fast-paced world; success and peace of mind are not found in the striving of Type A, nor in Type B's accepting things as they are, often awash in self-pity and the "I am the victim" excuse.

## Who's in Control?

Every one of life's haunting, worrisome questions—Who am I? Who cares about me? Why am I not where I should be? What am I heading for in the future?—takes on new meaning when we settle the question of "Who's in control?" When these questions assault us, the past shoves its way into the picture. How we deal with this baggage determines the weight of our worries and whether this stress becomes chronic.

Only the God of the Bible—not the Type A rat race—can help us handle guilt, frustration, or remorse. Only Jesus, God who became flesh—not the Type B complacency—can give us the true picture of who we are and how to make the most of the present. The stress-free life is the result of understanding what the good news has been telling people since the Garden of Eden. More than pills, more than another move or change (jobs, spouses, homes, etc.), the good news settles the basic question of relationships—with God first and then with others.

In summary, life's stresses are signals that not everything is in balance. Chronic stress is a result of focusing on the shallow, the artificial, the temporary. Chronic stress is a prison. Only the eternal strength of the great Caring One can liberate us and give us the long view, the strength for enduring, and a song in the heart. Here's His promise: "I have come in order that you might have life—life in all its fullness" (John 10:10, TEV).

---

**U.S. News & World Report,* Mar. 21, 1977.

# Chapter Seven

# Survivors Work Their Plan

Charles Schwab, founder and first president of both the United States Steel Corporation and the Bethlehem Steel Corporation, said that the simple technique of planning his daily schedule helped him to make more than $100 million (before modern inflation ruined the dollar)! He learned the technique from a successful friend who told him that he could give Schwab something that would increase his productivity 50 percent.

His friend handed Schwab a blank piece of paper and said, "Write on this paper the six most important tasks you have to do tomorrow. Number them in the order of their importance. First thing in the morning, look at item 1 and work on it until it is finished. Then tackle item 2 in the same way, and then all the rest. Don't be concerned if you have finished only one or two. Keep working on the most important. If you can't finish them all by this method, you couldn't have with any other method. Try it as long as you wish, and then send me a check for what you think it is worth."

Several weeks later Schwab sent his friend a check for $25,000. In his covering letter Schwab said that that simple lesson in daily planning was the most profitable advice he had ever received.

One of the first lessons that achieving persons learn is the value of a daily plan. Before going to bed at night, list the next day's duties. For me, this seems to organize my mind so that I can sleep comfortably. Often a thought comes during the night of something that I forgot to put on that list. If I had not made the list, I wouldn't have remembered what I had forgotten!

But this nighttime list is on top of the weekly plan that I make on Sunday or Monday. If I didn't know a week in advance what I should be doing each day of the coming week, I would be a basket case. But that nighttime list pulls together the latest telephone calls or e-mail messages that must be answered, or the incidentals around the house that must be done or bought. Again, priorities must be established even for that nighttime list.

Survivors also have a monthly plan. And a yearly one. And for the next five years. Soon the survivor will feel comfortable with their future. Worry is greatly reduced. If surprises come, and they will, it is easier to work everything in if there is a basic plan. Otherwise, life would be a constant battering, with no sense of accomplishing anything. Survivors will be no better than their plans; plans make the survivors.

### Visualizing Your Plan

Many are the examples of mental imaging producing the wanted results. Visualizing new attitudes or habits is often as important as actually practicing these habits! Mental practice helps us to improve and perfect right attitudes and right habits.

Many research projects have proven, for example, that one can improve the aim of throwing darts at a target by sitting in front of a dartboard and *mentally* throwing the darts. The same goes for improving basketball skills. One group practiced throwing the ball at the basket for 20 days. Another group never practiced. The third group spent 20 minutes daily for 20 days *imagining* that they were hitting the basket, in addition to actual practice. When they missed, they mentally corrected their aim! Each group was scored on the first and twentieth day. The first group improved 24 percent. The second showed no improvement. The third, which visualized their successful performances, improved 23 percent!*

Well-known golf and tennis instructors make sizable incomes teaching their clients to visualize successful swings while they are seated in a comfortable chair. Ben Hogan, one of the greatest golfers ever, calls his mental rehearsals "muscle memory."

## Law of Beholding

Apply this idea to your plans for your future. What kind of person do you want to be? Decisive, compassionate, gentle but firm? Let the law of beholding operate in your life: By beholding, we become changed. We become like the person we admire most. The apostle Paul said it well: "But we all, . . . beholding as in a mirror the glory of the Lord, are being transformed into the same image from glory to glory, just as by the Spirit of the Lord" (2 Cor. 3:18, NKJV).

Of course,. visualization takes time. So do mistakes and failures. Contrary to much of the positive mental attitude (PMA) of self-help books we are smothered with these days, it takes more than faith in oneself to do better tomorrow. Even more than merely imagining yourself successful. To be truly successful we need help from a higher Source.

Christians will contemplate the life of Christ and the life of mentors and models who have been truly successful people. Watch how generous these people are with their time, how resilient they are with disappointments, how kind they are to the young and those much older, how persistent they are in seeking God's daily presence and strength.

But alongside the law of beholding is the law of application. It was one thing for Einstein to visualize and to review mentally all the possibilities inherent in his blockbuster formula, $E=mc^2$. But the theoretical formula had to be worked out in practical physics to create the atomic bomb. Only when the "vision" is worked out in life will the law of beholding be effectual. Dreamers are great, but those who put their dreams to work are the leaders and the survivors.

The law of expression and impression is as inviolate as the law of gravity. To make the vision a reality, one must express the vision in word and action. With each expression, the impression deepens, and the easier it will be to make the next expression of perseverance, honesty, kindness, or whatever trait you have envisioned yourself as having. Such is the way great and eternal habits are formed. First the "beholding," then the application in words and deeds of what made that person worth beholding.

**Decisiveness, the Art of Making a Difference**

We learn the art of decisiveness by watching decisive people and sharing their habits. We become decisive and thus a person in great demand by following very clear basic habits: (1) Listen carefully; (2) probe for facts by raising thoughtful questions; (3) evaluate the information gathered.

The quality of decisiveness begins with right information correctly evaluated—the marks of a survivor. With sufficient information, decisive people exhibit certain valuable traits:

- Crispness in speech, conduct, attitudes, and conclusions. Not sharp or rude, but crisp.
- Positiveness, not arrogance, regarding themselves, their environment, and their values.
- Calm detachment regarding themselves and circumstances, because they think long-range.

The art of decisiveness grows with basic habits such as:

- Continue to gather and evaluate facts about whatever matter requires a decision. It could be some land for your home or investment, a new car, or a religious conviction.
- Become an expert in something. Homemakers, employees, entrepreneurs, teachers, administrators—everyone can become an expert in some area. Be good at what you do, and you will be in demand.

- Learn fundamentals of public speaking, not to be a great orator but for the simple reason that communication skills are at the roots of decisiveness.
- Continue to value your time by sticking close to your daily, weekly, and monthly plans. Distractions blur one's focus, and decisiveness unravels.

## The Art of Following "the Plan" Regardless of Critics

No one enjoys going cross-grained with colleagues, coworkers, or family members. Most people, even those with great ideas and personal commitment, give in when it seems that pressing one's opinion would bring ridicule, scorn, even rejection and the loss of a job.

But the world is immeasurably better off because of men and women who have good reason to swim against the current. President Theodore Roosevelt put it this way: "It is not the critic who counts; not the man who points out how the strong man stumbled, or where the doer of deeds could have done them better. The credit belongs to the man who is actually in the arena, whose face is marred by dust and sweat and blood; who strives valiantly; who errs and comes short again and again; who knows the great enthusiasms, the great devotions; who spends himself in a worthy cause; who, at the best, knows in the end the triumph of high achievement, and who, at the worst, if he fails, at least fails while daring greatly, so that his place shall never be with those timid souls who know neither victory nor defeat."

I think of those two Australian physicians who in

the 1980s proposed that bacteria called *H. pylori* was a common cause of ulcers. But according to the director of the Institute for Genome Research, "they were treated as village idiots." This discovery that bacteria cause stomach ulcers was one of the most amazing medical breakthroughs of this generation. For many years the medical world blamed stress, coffee, spicy foods, or too much stomach acid for ulcers—but no longer. (Aspirin and some other painkillers are the only major exceptions.) Question: What would the world of suffering men, women, and children still be like if those two Australian physicians had not kept pressing their findings in spite of the ridicule of their medical colleagues?

Such has been the history of the world. For nearly two millennia people believed Aristotle when he said that the heavier an object, the faster it would fall to earth. But in 1589 Galileo, as the story goes, summoned Aristotelian university professors to the base of the Tower of Pisa. He took two objects, weighing 10 pounds and one pound respectively, to the top of the tower and dropped them simultaneously. Both landed at the same time. Yet so committed were these learned men to their presuppositions and to their reputations that they denied what they had seen!

Do you believe ardently in something, regardless of general opinion? Is it something that you believe you can accomplish, though friends and even family believe you are wasting your time? It may be a clear expression of biblical truth that cuts across the grain of prevailing thought. After sound research, survivors keep their eyes on what they believe to be true, regardless of what others settle for. That clear eye, that unclouded personal mission statement, drives the survivor into the future with energy and inner joy.

### The High Dividends of Perseverance

Enthusiasm, visualization, and decisiveness are core components of the survivor's attitude. Without them, a person is ultimately a loser. But perseverance makes enthusiastic people into winners and, ultimately, survivors. The stories are legendary of famous men and women who broke free from frustration, even failure, by holding on a little longer. One example is Thomas Edison and his invention of the electric lightbulb.

If there is anything that I repeat more often to my grown-up children and their children, or to most any group I am asked to speak to, it is the simple plea "Never give up!" I have watched many commendable projects begun with much enthusiasm, many energetic young salespersons, many enthusiastic married couples, many excited students—but so many become discouraged "dropouts." They may be 90-day wonders—but watch out for day 91!

We all have occasions when we feel like giving up, that we are failures. I think of a man who indeed appeared to be a loser. At 14 he dropped out of school and hit the road. He tried odd jobs as a farmhand and hated it. At 16 he lied about his age and joined the Army—and hated that, too. When his one-year hitch was up he headed for Alabama and tried blacksmithing, and failed.

At 18 he got married, and within months his wife announced she was pregnant. On the same day he told her that he'd been fired—again. Then one day while he was job-hunting, his young wife gave away all their belongings and returned to her parents.

But he kept trying. While working at a succession of railroad jobs, he tried studying law by correspondence but dropped out. He tried selling insurance, selling tires, running a service station—but nothing for long.

Too soon he was 65 years old. The years had slid by, a lifetime nearly gone and nothing to show for it. He had had it. The United States government sent his first pension check and told him he was "old."

But something inside him seemed to explode. He took his first pension check of $105 and started a new business. And the new business clicked! The man who failed at everything except one thing—the man who never gave up—was Harland Sanders—Colonel Harland Sanders. The business he started with his first Social Security check was Kentucky Fried Chicken!

I also think of the shortest commencement address ever given. Sir Winston Churchill, aging and sickly, was asked to give the commencement address at Oxford University. Churchill tottered to the podium. Hanging his cane on the desk, he peered at his young audience through his thick, bushy eyebrows, set his famous jaw, and exclaimed, "Never give up!"

He took a step backward and again surveyed those eager young faces. Reaching into that great, inner reservoir of personal experience, Sir Winston's legendary voice rose in intensity, "Never give up!"

After an extra long pause, he roared, "Never give up!"

Then he took his cane and shuffled back to his seat. Stunned, the graduates sat in silence. Then the applause began, and ended in a thunderous, standing ovation for the old lion.

Sir Winston Churchill had delivered the briefest commencement address on record but perhaps the most memorable. It summed up his remarkable life, "Never give up!" If he had given up during the 1930s when most of his government colleagues had rejected him as irrelevant and a "has-been," we would never have heard the voice that most people say saved the free world in the 1940s.

The remarkable career of Cal Ripken, Jr., continues to challenge sportsmen everywhere. On September 5, 1995, he tied Lou Gehrig's legendary record of playing in 2,130 consecutive games. The sellout crowd at Baltimore's Oriole Park at Camden Yards gave him a standing ovation for five minutes and 20 seconds. But the next evening, when he eclipsed that record, the ovation lasted an amazing 22 minutes and 15 seconds. Moreover, he continued extending his record through the summer of 1998, ending on September 20 with 2,632 games played!

But the Ripken name stands for more than iron-man endurance. Respect for Ripken builds on his unsullied character, which reflects his life plan of doing his best and doing it repeatedly in a world in which people get their publicity with so much less. Ripken is a survivor for all the reasons that we are discussing in this book.

No one seems to understand the load you're carrying? Maybe, but don't give up!

You see no way out of the troubles at home? You may not, but God does. Don't give up!

You feel as if you're working your socks off and no one seems to recognize it? Perhaps, but don't give up!

You just learned that you have a sickness that may suddenly change all the plans for your future? Possibly, but don't give up!

Survivors survive because they hang on a little longer than others. And other people hang on to survivors because they can be trusted!

---

*Maxwell Maltz, *Psycho-Cybernetics* (New York: Pocket Books, 1966), pp. 27-42.

# Chapter Eight

# Survivors Are Creatures of Habit

If anything, survivors are creatures of habit. But habits cannot be measured like muscle or observed on an electrocardiogram.

"Habit" is a word that describes what happens when thoughts or acts are repeated. Habits are truly good friends! Think of the time we save when we tie our shoes, drive cars, or use the typewriter or computer, by not having to consciously consider each movement! Remember the hours and weeks it took to develop these skills?

Habits are our built-in survival kit. To the extent wholesome habits control our lives, to that extent we enjoy life. I don't mean that they ensure full-time happiness, but we can live with great peace about the bigger issues of life—all the time. If we are not enjoying life, we may be plugged into the wrong habit systems.

How are habits made or unmade? Wise Solomon said that as a man thinks, "so is he" (Prov. 23:7). We think with brain cells that lie an inch behind our forehead. These brain cells are the capital of the body, the power center for all that happens to every nerve and muscle. The brain's messages are sent "electrically" at astonishing speeds that scientists have not yet been able to replicate on the most advanced computer.

Most of the illnesses that physicians see in their offices are mentally or emotionally induced (psychosomatic). We have all experienced the truth of this fact: when our willpower is at low ebb, when the mind or emotions wrestle with bad news, we have difficulty resisting a cold or an upset stomach. But this same principle can be changed around. With habits of positive attitudes and trust in God, our bodies respond to our thoughts, and we can resist disease and overcome illnesses.

How does the brain do this work? The entire brain operates on 10 watts of electricity and performs math calculations that far outrun the world's largest computers. Each brain cell has many fibers called dendrites, which receive all kinds of information constantly. One long fiber called an axon transmits messages between cells.

A microscope shows that on the end of each axon are tiny enlargements called boutons (French for "buttons"). These boutons secrete chemicals (ACH and GABA), which stimulate the next cell to send a message down the nerve path to whatever muscle or organ is to be activated. But there is no direct connection between the axon and the next cell's dendrites, only a tiny space, called the synapse. How does the message get across this synapse? Through the chemicals of the boutons.

### Thoughts and Acts Make Boutons

Here is where it gets interesting: some axons have more boutons than others. Why? Because that axon has been stimulated by certain thoughts or actions more than other axons. More stimulation, more boutons. With more boutons, the easier it is the next time for similar messages to flow along that particular pathway. Habits are forming!

How, then, are boutons formed? Any thought or action forms a bouton. Thoughts and acts often repeated build more boutons on the end of that particular axon, so that it becomes easier to repeat that same thought or action when the same situation is again faced. Just as cutting across the lawn eventually wears a worn path, so repeated thoughts actually produce physical and chemical changes in our nerve pathways. Thoughts don't vanish into thin air; they are etched into a biochemical pattern that we call habits.

The good news and the bad news is that boutons never disappear. Right! Frightening as well as assuring! For example, recovered alcoholics tell each other that they "are always" alcoholics. So they avoid friends who drink and places where alcoholic beverages are likely to be distributed. Chocoholics and those involved in "fatal attractions" never lose those boutons that made it easy for them to "cave in."

But the good news is that the bad-habit boutons can be overpowered by good-habit boutons. Those who find it easy to be angry or to be lazy or to be self-centered can be assured that with the right set of the mind and the power of God, new habits of self-control, industriousness, and caring can be established firmly. *We are what we think.*

Sounds too easy? Here is how we build more yes or no boutons, whichever is appropriate for the occasion. For example, if we are used to saying "Yes" to bad choices, we must build "No" boutons.

## Habits Changed in Weeks

Research indicates that we can change most any habit in a matter of weeks—some say 21 days! When we choose to resist temptation (that is, whatever is not in our best, long-range interests), when we say "No!" the GABA secretion is secreted at the synapse. GABA puts the brakes on and keeps that cell from firing. With repeated resistance (repeated "No's") more "No" boutons are formed. With more "No" boutons on the end of that axon that had formerly led to inappropriate sexual behavior or quick anger, GABA (the brake) is even more powerful, making it virtually impossible to do wrong in that particular situation again.

Sound too simple? There is a warning. The GABA secretion does not function well, most often not at all, when we lose sleep or get fatigued for whatever reason, good or bad. GABA (the brake on our decision-making) is affected by fatigue much sooner than ACH (the accelerator on our decision-making). That is, when we are tired we find it easier to do and say what we please, long after we have lost our braking power. That is why committee meetings in the evenings, Saturday night flings, and nighttime confrontations with others (children, spouses) most often turn into regrettable experiences. When we are tired the go-for-it, tell-it-like-it-is, have-fun attitude has no GABA to say no!

To get even more practical, most of life is a matter of conflicting choices—shall I, or shall I not? One brain cell says, "Why not? Go for it!" The other says, "No, you'd better not!" Which one wins? The one with the most boutons built up by habit! One brain cell sees the extra piece of scrumptious pecan pie or the banana sundae; or the possibility of getting a better grade by cheating because everyone is doing it; or eating between meals and skipping breakfast; or undue familiarity with the opposite sex. However, another brain cell becomes activated; it sees the same opportunities and says, "No, there's a better way. I choose to be a survivor; all those negative habits will keep me from my full potential. I want to honor my parents (or my spouse, or my God). I want to be trusted."

All this choosing—this mental activity—takes electrical energy. The brain cell that has the most boutons on its axon has the most electrical energy and wins! When negative temptation of any kind says "Go for it! Looks good; take a piece," or "Go for it; no one will ever know," 30 millivolts, shall we say, of ACH energy surges into your action cell. But your better self says (if you are not in fatigue), "Hold it, there are consequences down the road I don't want to live with. Don't fire! [that is, "Don't cheat," "Don't take that extra piece, etc."]." If the better brain cell has more boutons, GABA jumps into action with 40 millivolts, shall we say, of electrical power, saying "No!" Because it takes only 10 millivolts for a cell to fire, the brain cell with the most boutons wins![1]

Let's consider this again! All it takes to say no *when you should* is a difference of 10 millivolts of electrical power. The brain cell is making a fast algebraic decision in a matter of a thousandth of a second—and the 10 extra millivolts will make the difference.

This is how survivor habits are formed. More boutons (because of the same thoughts and actions repeated often) equal more electric current to say no or yes at the proper times. The more boutons producing a certain habit pattern, the more spontaneous, habitual, and natural will be the ability to make right decisions in the future. That is how right decisions form right habits that form right characters.

The eminent Harvard psychologist William James observed: "Could the young but realize how soon they will become mere walking bundles of habits, they would give more heed to their conduct while in the plastic state. We are spinning our fates, good or evil, and never to be undone. Every smallest stroke of virtue or vice leaves its never-so-little scar. . . . The drunken Rip Van Winkle, in Jefferson's play, excuses himself for every fresh dereliction by saying, 'I won't count this time!' Well! He may not count it, and a kind Heaven may not count it; but it is being counted nonetheless. Down among his nerve cells and fibers the molecules are counting it, registering and storing it up to be used against him when the next temptation comes. Nothing we ever do, in strict scientific literalness, is wiped out.

"Of course, this has its good side as well as its bad one. As we become permanent drunkards by so many separate drinks, so we become saints in the moral, and authorities and experts in the practical and scientific spheres, by so many separate acts and hours of work."[2]

However, the survivor remembers that negative habits are always there in the shadows, because all boutons remain in place. We may repent and set our feet in right paths, but familiarity with the former temptations is a crease in the paper that cannot be completely unfolded. That is why wise Paul could say, "Let him who thinks he stands take heed lest he fall" (1 Cor. 10:12, NKJV).

At this point, at this crucial knife edge of each person's future on which all else balances, we must be very clear and honest with ourselves: Willpower, no matter how strong, will never be sufficient to build enough boutons so that we will be above temptation. Furthermore, survivors know they live in a very dynamic universe, and forces beyond the human are impressing us constantly.

Only by the empowering of the personal intervention of the Holy Spirit, the Eternal Energy of the universe, can any of us be prompted even to begin wanting to make the right boutons along the right axons. Even God chooses not to make the right boutons for us, or fire up our decision-making, if we do not *choose* His way. This choosing is the first step in making new boutons. *God does not choose for us any more than He does our breathing for us!* But He has wired us to succeed with a neural system that defies human imagination or duplication. All He wants from us is our choice. Each right choice becomes another bouton, until the "weight" of boutons forms a strong and good habit.

Through it all, God stands ready day and night, holding before us the reasons that we should choose His way of making sense out of our lives. He never wearies, providing the electrical energy that jump-starts our electrical system whenever we choose to plug into His power. And He never gives up on us, even if we fail again and again in the self-correcting process of reaching our goals. He is already there to jump-start us again with more energy to make more boutons of the right kind. That is what Paul meant when he said, "God is at work in you, both to will and to work for his good pleasure" (Phil. 2:13, RSV).

The good news is that the more we get in the practice of permitting the Lord to help us say yes to His plans for us, the easier it becomes to keep adding boutons on the right axons. That is why we must make a habit of focusing on those things that are true, honest, just, pure, lovely, and of a good report, as Paul put it so eloquently (see Phil. 4:8). Each act of focusing becomes a new bouton until what one focuses on becomes a fixed habit and is reflected in the survivor's own experience. That is why the survivor can rest in quiet assurance that faithfulness in doing today's duties and homework will play out in competency tomorrow. That is the steady tread of survivors as they walk into the future.

---

[1] Elden M. Chalmers and Esther L. Chalmers, *Making the Most of Family Living* (Mountain View, Calif.: Pacific Press Pub. Assn., 1979), pp. 61-67.

[2] *Ibid.*, pp. 66, 67.

Chapter Nine

# Survivors Discover the Power of Hope

Hope is to the human spirit what air is to the lungs. We seem to appreciate air and hope more when we lose them than when we have them! When was the last time you thought about breathing? But when you are not getting enough air, you surely know something is wrong. The same is true about hope.

But after saying the obvious, I find it worth noting that the dwindling of hope is one of the least recognized, and perhaps the least talked about, human experiences. When facing adversity we are told to "keep a stiff upper lip," or bluster through it. Besides, we hesitate to burden others with what may be termed negative thinking. But the death of hope is not an unusual phenomenon. Jeremiah put it this way: "I have been deprived of peace; I have forgotten what prosperity is. So I say, 'My splendor [or strength] is gone and all that I had hoped from the Lord'" (Lam. 3:17, 18, NIV). At some time in the lives of all of us we may understand well what Jeremiah is describing.

Have you ever said something like this: "All the work I do doesn't seem to matter." "Nothing seems worth it anymore." "My energy level is not what it used to be." "I feel so unfulfilled." "How long do I have to put up with this?" "Why bother? Who cares?" "Will it ever end?" All such feelings arise when hope fades.

One doesn't spot a no-hoper by a high cholesterol count, or by exploding blood pressure, or by excessive weight. Many people with these problems are having the time of their lives, to hear them talk. Many mask their real fears and dark thoughts with substitute gratifications. Often the life of the party, they mirror many of the world's comedians and movie stars who hide their fears and anxieties with their jokes and high living.

Besides suicide, another devastating indication of the loss of hope is alcoholism or drug addiction. Or the credit-card binge. Or serial marriages. Or refrigerator raids. When hope fades, many try to eliminate an intolerable, suffocating future by fleeing reality, by filling the void with instant gratification.

This kind of thinking breaks down the immune system—probably faster than any other cause. No-hopers invite all kinds of physical ailments, beginning with the common cold. This kind of thinking feeds on itself and becomes self-fulfilling. We soon become the kind of people we think we are. Or what others have told us we are: losers, second-rate, human trash, terminal cases. All of these thoughts may have nothing to do with reality, but without hope they surely become reality fast.

A professor of cardiology at the Harvard Medical

School tells of an experience he had as a young resident physician. His patient was a middle-aged librarian who had a narrowing of one of the valves on the right side of her heart, the tricuspid valve. She was suffering from a low-grade congestive heart failure. With digitalis medication she was maintaining her job efficiently, as well as her home duties. She had been closely monitored for 10 years—everything had been kept under control.

One time when she came in for her checkup, the chief cardiologist greeted her warmly. He turned to his entourage of bright, young resident physicians and said: "This woman has TS," and abruptly left her with the other physicians.

As soon as the chief cardiologist left the room the pleasant librarian's attitude changed abruptly. She appeared anxious and frightened. She began to breathe rapidly, clearly hyperventilating. Her skin became drenched with perspiration, and her pulse accelerated to more than 150 beats per minute.

The young resident began to examine her immediately. To his astonishment, her lungs, which a few minutes earlier had been clear, now had moist crackles at the bases.

He questioned his patient as to the reasons for her sudden upset. Her response was that she had heard the chief cardiologist say that she had TS, which she knew meant "terminal situation."

Although the young physician was amused at her misinterpretation of the medical acronym for "tricuspid stenosis," he soon became very apprehensive himself. She wouldn't believe his soothing words! After all, she had heard "the truth" from the man who had been treating her for 10 years!

In a very short while she was in massive pulmonary edema. Heroic measures on the part of probably the best team of physicians in the world could not reverse her frothing congestion. That afternoon she died from heart failure. She had lost hope!

This kind of story can be repeated many times—either for the positive or negative turn, whether it be physical, mental, emotional, or spiritual. Many stories can be told of people who have astonished the medical world with their physical recovery, chiefly because of the power of hope. We know that in recent years physicians have been using "blocking" medications to protect the heart from erratic rhythms or to intercept severe pain in joints or muscles or to modify the brain chemistry in mental illness. The same is true for hope and gratitude; they are observable agents for blocking the effects of panic, anxiety, and depression.

Hope has a way of releasing endorphins when even heavy exercise fails. A vegetarian diet and jogging 10 miles a day may fall short of reversing physical and mental spinouts. But hope is often the bulletproof vest that protects us against the effects of emotional assaults.

I think of Aleksandr Solzhenitsyn—that remarkable survivor of the worst of times. He made the word "gulag" famous in the Western world. Imprisoned for years in Russian prisons because of his courageous stand against Communist powers, he survived literally on hope.

For long periods of time the prisoners were not

allowed even to speak! Further, they were forbidden to read. Solzhenitsyn said that the strain and repression became overwhelming. He thought, *I will never get out of here.* So he planned how he would end his life. He knew that if he tried to escape, he would be shot; and, he wrote, "that would be the end of that."

The next day he was taken, as usual, with the other prisoners out to work. When a break came, he sat down under a tree. He even placed his hand against the tree, ready to push off and run. He would be shot, and out of his misery. Just then a shadow came across the grass. A fellow prisoner sat down beside him. Although forbidden to speak, he could at least look into the eyes of other prisoners. The two men locked eyes. Solzhenitsyn saw something he had rarely seen in any face—a message of love and concern.

Then the other prisoner took a step forward, and with a stick in his hand drew a cross in the sand. New hope surged. Thoughts of God flooded Solzhenitsyn's mind: *God has not forsaken me. He loves me. He is in charge.* For weary Solzhenitsyn there was still hope, and he would live on.

Would you believe, three days later, without any warning, he was released from that prison? At his release he learned that many people had been praying for him. He knew there was reason to hope.

And so he did, giving us some of the greatest literature of the twentieth century. Solzhenitsyn has been credited as one of the most potent forces that brought Communism down. He was truly saved by hope (Rom. 8:24). Hope is very powerful.

But there are other prisons besides those created by

wire and stone. The prison for some is a seemingly impossible personal handicap. I think of Wilma Rudolph, the first American woman to win three Olympic gold medals in track and field, back in 1960. What most people don't know is that Wilma was born a loser, not a winner, with all the marks of a no-hoper.

She was born a preemie, contracted double pneumonia twice, and was crippled by polio—all this in her earliest years! Her left leg was bent, her foot twisted inward. She wore braces from age 5 through 11, and traveled weekly to Nashville for treatments. But though her leg was in steel, her mind soared, dreaming of running and playing like other children. She had the makings of a survivor!

To make her dreams come true, to grab the power of hope, whenever her parents left the house she took off her leg brace and practiced walking, painfully, one step at a time, until she could make her way across the room. At age 11 she decided to confess to her physician and parents what she had been doing. When the amazed physician saw her shuffle around his office, he agreed that she could take the braces off now and then at home. That was all Wilma needed to hear. She took off her braces and never put them on again!

Hope in her heart mixed with determination. In fact, that is the only way hope works. Hope without determination is only wishful thinking. So Wilma began to run with her school friends. In high school she set new records. In 1960 she pounded down the track in Rome to win three gold medals, each of them in world-record time. Wilma turned iron braces into

Olympic gold. She tapped into the power of hope—a real survivor!

Another prison that too often eclipses hope is emotional wounds, either self-inflicted or caused by letting other people suck hope out of our lives. Many people have been unconsciously programmed by others to aim too low, to sell themselves short. How does that happen? In ways that are almost too painful to mention. So many have been told for so long by somebody—perhaps their parents, or grandparents, or schoolteachers—that they are as "slow as molasses," or "clumsy as an elephant," or "always the sick one in the family," or they "never finish what they start," or by their spouses that they are "lousy lovers." The sad list goes on.

Such people go through life thinking that they are truly no better than what others have said they are. Beyond this verbal abuse, so many live with the dark, ugly memory of physical and sexual abuse. Their self-perception of these toxic events has made them feel no better than human trash. These deep emotional scars affect almost every human relationship they enter for the rest of their lives. They really believe that they are what others have made them out to be. The thought that they could possibly be better or different rarely arises. They live in a gray fog of accepting the lie about themselves, so why try? "Why try another hairstyle—who cares?" "Why take a self-improvement class?" "Why forgo present pleasures for future good?" "Who cares if I pull up my socks?" Have you heard those words before? They come when hope is slipping.

Another way people set themselves up for these

self-inflicted wounds is to believe that they are victims of fate, or of circumstances they can't control. Especially regarding illnesses, we hear, "Oh, I always catch everything going around." "My son gave it to me." Or "It runs in the family." Or "I don't know how I got it!"

On bigger issues we hear, "This is the way we've always done it! Nothing will change!" From so many adults—"My parents have never said I've done anything right!" "My boss always plays favorites!" "I'm just not good enough!"

This kind of thinking brings great relief for the moment—because it shifts responsibility. By thinking this way we escape making responsible decisions. So we hear, "I can't do anything about it." It's like taking an emotional aspirin to cut down the pain of personal responsibility.

But this kind of thinking invites deadly consequences. We make ourselves into victims rather than responsible people. And the twilight of hope only darkens. *The fundamental question is How do we supplant anxiety or victimitis with hope?*

There are two ways of looking into the future—with anxiety or with hope. Without hope, we face the future without air in our spiritual lungs. Despair is near, inviting the "paralysis of intellectual and spiritual powers by a feeling of senselessness and purposelessness of existence."*

Hope or anxiety is the way we live in the future today. Hope or anxiety is not a mere passive way of looking at the future; our present life is affected directly.

One way to avoid anxiety is to attempt to control

it, to have a kind of power over the future. How do people tend to do this? By adding to financial wealth. By concentrating on having the "right" friends in high places. How many well-known people end up in despair or in the suicide statistics, surrounded by their wealth and their idolizing friends!

Survivors think differently. They realize that there is nothing that we can do, by ourselves, to guarantee the circumstances of the future. So they prepare for the unknown today. They understand that we all can think of short-range hopes and long-range hopes. I think of my days on a tractor during an early pastorate, plowing the rich Illinois soil on the church deacon's farm. How does one plow a straight furrow? By visually lining up a point at the front end of the tractor with a marker at the far end, perhaps on a tree or fence post. Survivors keep their eyes on short-range goals and on long-range goals at the same time. That double focus grows hope.

Consider some short-range goals: the farmer sows, the teacher teaches, the business person ventures money and equity. They all hope that something good will come out of all this down payment on the future. In other words, the picture of the future sets in motion the powers of the present—the power of hope!

Long-range hopes focus on how we would like to spend our mature years, how helpful we can be to loved ones, to neighbors, and to everyone else we touch in some way, how weak or strong our old age will be, and what happens after death. The chief question real survivors ask is not where they will be in five years but, rather, where they will be 5,000 years from now!

Some would say that we need not worry about these long-range hopes—what will happen will happen. They muddle through the present with their short-range goals as if long-range hopes don't matter. But that is precisely the problem for so many. Living with only short-range hopes produces the deep anxieties that color the present. No matter how much is in the bank, or how exotic the vacations, parties, drugs, or whatever—there is always that shadow over it all. Lurking in the shadows are those dreaded thoughts: *It may not last. Someone will take it from me. Why is it that I am not satisfied? Isn't there something better?* And so the search goes on for increased emphasis on all these diversions, ratcheting up their instant gratifications.

Human beings were made to see life as a whole; they were not made to live in the present only. The wise man said that God placed "eternity into man's mind" (Eccl. 3:11, RSV). Much of today's distress is caused basically by a lack of hope—an unclear understanding of the big picture called life. A stress-free life is simply a life that lives with hope—not irrationally, not irresponsibly, but realistically. Such is the mental framework of the survivor.

During an important baseball game, Willard Hershberger, catcher for the Cincinnati Reds, signaled a wrong pitch. The batter hit a home run that cost the Reds the game. Hershberger worried about his mistake for days. He hardly spoke to anyone. He didn't smile; he paced the floor at night. No one could snap him out of his deepening depression. On August 2, 1940, Hershberger did not come to the ballpark. He was found in his room, dead from his own hand—a no-hoper with no long-range goals that would put the present in perspective.

But think of Jeff Blatnick, the superheavyweight gold medal winner of Greco-Roman wrestling in the 1984 Olympics. He knew what it meant to get up and to keep on keeping on, in spite of day-to-day hardships. Along with the extremely stressful practices necessary to get on the Olympic team, he discovered that he had Hodgkin's disease. No one gave him much chance. At the victory press conference following his triumph, he said: "It's been the story of my life. Something sets me back, and I bounce back harder than ever."

Also in 1984 Joan Benoit won the U.S. women's Olympic marathon trials only 17 days after undergoing arthroscopic knee surgery! When asked how she managed to get through the trials, she replied, "I just never gave up."

For issues much more important than winning in the Olympics, the resolve to never give up, the spirit of hope, is absolutely fundamental to a happy, healthy, holy, stress-free life—no matter what the problems or personal prisons we must deal with.

Caution: A positive mental attitude that is based on human effort and willpower will never be sufficient. It will let you down sooner or later. But a positive mental attitude based on the willingness of God to forgive our past, to strengthen us to carry well every present challenge, and to give us the reality of a future that will always be better than our past—that kind of mental attitude will move mountains.

That is why God, our best friend, wants us to be

very clear about the nature of hope. Without hope we asphyxiate ourselves, either physically or spiritually. Perhaps that is the special reason Bible writers refer to the second coming of Jesus as "the blessed hope" (Titus 2:13, NIV). That blessed hope is part of a survivor's long-range plan. Furthermore, keeping that hope in view (like the faraway fence I kept looking at from my tractor) will infuse short-range goals with peace and steadiness amid the normal stress of just living.

Hope is the badge of the survivor. This is not some modern discovery, as one might think by reading the literature about positive mental attitudes (PMA). It is the basic message of the Judeo-Christian Scriptures. The psalmist sang: "Happy is he who has the God of Jacob for his help, whose hope is in the Lord his God" (Ps. 146:5, NKJV). The apostle Paul wrote, "We are saved by hope" (Rom. 8:24). In fact, the purpose of the Holy Scriptures is basically to provide hope for struggling, baffled humanity: "Everything written in the Scriptures was written to teach us, in order that we might have hope through the patience and encouragement which the Scriptures give us" (Rom. 15:4, TEV).

I know some are asking, "Don't even survivors at times feel weak, sometimes short on hope?" Of course they do. The light flickers for all at times. Ofttimes, the twilight descends very quickly—the loss of a "secure" job or of a loved one; rejection by parents, by a spouse, by a trusted friend, or by children. I have friends who were devastated by divorce, or by an engagement that suddenly fell through. For those dear friends, the light at the end of the tunnel seemed snuffed out overnight.

When that light dims, ordinary responsibilities often become too much. Things that once came so easily now become formidable. That is why the *power of hope* resting on biblical promises has cleared the tunnel of despair for millions through the years.

The biblical principle of hope as our life breath is found like a red thread throughout the Bible: For whatever the reason, "Hope deferred makes the heart sick" (Prov. 13:12, NKJV). "Anxiety in the heart of man causes depression, but a good word makes it glad" (Prov. 12:25, NKJV). Who hasn't experienced the truth of those words?

There are scores of biblical sentences that begin "Be not afraid," "Fret not," "Trust in the Lord," "Be anxious over nothing."

But a warning: Don't expect to feel the desire to "want" to read the Bible when the light flickers. It may be the last thing in the world you may *feel* like doing! Why? God seems far away. We find it easier either to wallow in self-pity or to find friends who seem only to increase our negative thinking. We all know the feeling. Regardless, start reading!

Where does one start? Try Psalms 23, 27, and 37. Or Proverbs 3. Or Luke 15 or 22. Or John 3 and 18-20. Or Philippians. Choose a modern translation, such as the *Good News Bible* or the New King James Version.

Slowly it will dawn that we are not the first to have troubles, nor the first to feel the bitterness of being let down by "trusted" friends or false dreams. Slowly we begin to realize that we are not the first to consider quitting. Then we realize that the Bible was written for people just like us.

Our source of hope is not in some wall motto or some quick, psychological Band-aid. Nor is it to be found even in the sympathy of a fellow human being. As noted earlier, hope is not a matter of wishful thinking or just one more attempt to drown out troubles. Hope is a matter of trusting the rules of the universe and the very reliable Person who stands behind all this great advice. Hope gives zest to life when we believe that the Lord of the universe will never forsake us. That's why we may get older but never old.

Hope is always best when grounded in a Person who can be trusted absolutely. When we are troubled with problems bigger than life, we need a Person bigger than our problems. That's why the psalmist could sing: "Trust in the Lord, and do good; dwell in the land, and feed on His faithfulness. Delight yourself also in the Lord, and He shall give you the desires of your heart" (Ps. 37:3, 4, NKJV).

Survivors truly affirm the truth that we are "saved by hope." Yet even hope fades, no matter how much we hope, *if we do not sense that there is indeed meaning to life.* Survivors hope in times of great crisis but not foolishly—they have discovered that life does have meaning. Hope always fades when life's meaning becomes vague. In our next chapter we will take a long look at how to find meaning in life.

---

*Emil Brunner, *Eternal Hope* (Philadelphia: Westminster Press, 1954), p. 7.

Chapter Ten

# Survivors Find Meaning to Life

Charles Colson wrote a fascinating book called *Loving God,* in which he relates one of the most fantastic stories I've ever heard.[1]

He tells of a Jewish Russian physician. He had been sentenced to a gulag, the dreaded Russian concentration camp. We don't know what his crime was, except that it was political. Now, to be a Jewish physician in the Soviet Union suggests that he must have been in sympathy with Communism. After all, most of the Jews in the Soviet Union fell in with Communism for a very simple reason: For more than 200 years they had been persecuted by professed Christians, with the blessing of the czars. A glimpse of their misery may be gained from the unforgettable film *Fiddler on the Roof.*

One of the top officials in the Christian church in Russia once said, "We need to kill one third of the Jews, imprison another third, and see that the other one third leave the country." Against that backdrop, you can see why Communism would appear to Jews as salvation from Christian oppression.

So it must have appeared to Boris Nicholayevich Kornfield, M.D. But at some point he apparently questioned Stalin and had been sentenced to the gulag. Reflect for a moment—physicians in a prison camp care for everyone, including the commander and the guards, as well as the other prisoners. Thus physicians are treated with deference in comparison with other prisoners. After all, who would want to go under the knife of a surgeon who hates you and might let you bleed to death as his knife slipped? So Boris must have enjoyed some favors other prisoners never saw.

One day he talked to a patient who said he was a Christian, that he believed the Bible, that he believed in God's Messiah, and that Messiah was a suffering Jew. The patient talked of his sufferings as being unworthy to compare with the sufferings of God's Messiah. But Boris had never felt he deserved any of the suffering he was going through. He had an intense hatred for Christians, for all that had been done in their Christ's name against his people.

Yet he saw in this man a quiet confidence and conviction he had seen in no one else. Very quietly, very secretly, Boris accepted Jesus Christ to be his Messiah.

Dr. Kornfield began to think about all the implications of this new commitment. He examined his own life. For instance, it was routine that before any prisoner could be put in solitary confinement, a physician had to sign a form and say he was physically in good shape—certificates that nearly always were lies. Most men died in solitary confinement—and he had signed hundreds of such forms.

But now Boris decided that as a Christian he

would no longer lie in preparing those forms. In this resolve not to lie, he knew he would be signing his own death warrant.

One day in the hospital ward Boris saw men dying of diseases from which they could have survived had they only had food! After seeing one such prisoner die he walked out into the hall, only to see an orderly, a turncoat prisoner, eating the bread that had been intended for the sick patients. Boris reported the orderly to the commandant.

The commandant was amused. "All right," he said, "we'll put the orderly in solitary confinement for three days." The compassionate physician knew that when that orderly got out of solitary he would be as good as dead.

One afternoon a few days later Boris Kornfield walked into his hospital ward and saw a patient who had just been operated on for cancer. He was used to seeing sorrow in faces, but there was a sorrow and a depth of sensitivity in this face that he had seen in no other prisoner. And so Boris sat beside this total stranger and poured out what had happened in his own life—how he was a Jew, how he had become disillusioned with Communism, how he had embraced God's Messiah, how he had seen that he could no longer sign the solitary confinement warrants, and how he knew he had only a very short time to live.

But he said, "I feel freer than any man in the Soviet Union, and I feel a joy I never knew existed." Here was developing the true spirit of the survivor who could triumph over circumstances—he was finding meaning to life.

What about that patient to whom Kornfield poured out his soul? He was in and out of consciousness in that recovery room as the anesthetic wore off. But he was fascinated by the physician's comments. He held on to every word. Somehow he stayed awake.

Later that night the recovering patient listened for the doctor to return as usual. Again the next morning he waited for this remarkable physician. But Dr. Boris Kornfield never returned. When he had left his patient that previous afternoon, as he stepped into the hall he was struck in the head eight times. He was dead the next day.

But the patient Dr. Kornfield had talked to was Aleksandr Solzhenitsyn, who learned the higher level of survival attitude from the converted Jew. Boris Kornfield finally found profound meaning to life, and that meaning was more important than the fear of death. From this Jewish physician Solzhenitsyn found new meaning to life and became the moral beacon who encouraged hundreds of thousands of fellow Russians to hold on a little longer. After his release from prison, Solzhenitsyn was eventually expelled from Russia because he spoke so loudly, so eloquently, against the inhumanity and meaninglessness of Communism.

Another remarkable book was written by Terrence Des Pres, entitled *The Survivor: An Anatomy of Life in the Death Camps.*[2] I had read many books that described the horrors of the most terrible years of the twentieth century, but this one went deeper. With scores of quotations from once-secret documents and personal interviews with death-camp survivors, Des

Pres drew a direct connection between staying alive and staying human. After describing the gross indecencies and hell of the camps, he speaks of the survivor as one who "manages to stay alive in body *and* in spirit, enduring dread and hopelessness without the loss of will to carry on in human ways."[3]

That's why Solzhenitsyn's literary contributions are so important, so instructive. His survivors "keep life and decency intact. . . . By choosing not only to live, but to live humanly, they take upon themselves the burden of an action requiring much will and courage, much clearsightedness and faith in life."[4]

This kind of conviction, that life matters, that somehow there is a meaning to life that transcends humanity's inhumanities, compelled Corrie ten Boom to be the extraordinary savior of many Jewish neighbors during the awful Nazi occupation of Holland. Even though she saw most of her family sent off to the death camps, even though she and her sister, Betsie, endured the unspeakable terror of Ravensbruck, Corrie could record Betsie's last whisper before she died in the camp: "[We] must tell people what we have learned here. We must tell them that there is no pit so deep that He is not deeper still. They will listen to us, Corrie, because we have been here."[5]

I know that I have raised more questions than I have answered. What kind of meaning can there be, for example, in a world in which sophisticated men and women can play Mozart while they kill men, women, and children by the millions? Why do babies die of leukemia or underdeveloped hearts? Why do tornadoes destroy this home and not that one?

What about John the Baptist, of whom Jesus said no one ever born was greater? He was only a young man when beheaded for his faith in his cousin, Jesus of Nazareth. But he died, even as Boris Kornfield died, with a great sense of meaning that transcended the horrors that surrounded him.

How do *we* find meaning to life, either when the sky is blue or in stormy times? We, too, must look at life at that point where Boris and John were, without the advantage of knowing how all the terror or disillusionment will play out in our lives. We must think as they did, as survivors who can see no further into the immediate future than anyone else.

I would not be so unwise as to define meaning for you. We each find meaning in very personal experiences that are difficult to describe, sensitive as they may be. But I can refer you to those broad, time-tested parameters in which meaning has been found through the centuries, and without which the night of meaninglessness closes in, sooner or later.

Martin E. P. Seligman, professor of psychology at the University of Pennsylvania, wrote one of the more remarkable books I have ever read, entitled *Learned Optimism*.[6] He linked depression with the loss of meaning. After much research, he believes that an inordinate, "unbridled" focus on self and/or the lack of social bonding lead to depression and that dark night of meaninglessness.

Listen to his counsel: "A society that exalts the individual to the extent ours now does will be riddled with depression. And as it becomes apparent that individualism produces a tenfold increase in depression, individualism will become a less appealing creed to live by. . . . One necessary condition for meaning is the attachment to something larger than you are. The larger the entity you can attach yourself to, the more meaning you can derive. To the extent that it is now difficult for young people to take seriously their relationship to God, to care about their duties to the country, or to be part of a large and abiding family, meaning in life will be very difficult to find. . . . The self, to put it another way, is a very poor site for meaning."[7]

Seligman traces the rise of the "modern" self, "the expansion of the self," in the twentieth century. He calls "this new self, with its absorbing concern for its gratifications and losses, the 'maximal' self to distinguish it from what it has replaced, the 'minimal,' or Yankee, self, the self our grandparents had. The Yankee self . . . did little more than just behave; it was certainly less preoccupied with how it felt. It was less concerned with feelings and more concerned with duty. . . . The waxing of the self in our time coincided with a diminished sense of community and loss of higher purpose. These together proved rich soil for depression to grow in."[8]

Profound simplicity! When the self is the center of one's universe, when self-gratification is the test of pleasure and happiness, when life's agenda is focused on self-preservation (with its ego-centered appeal for comfort, entertainment, and sexual satisfaction), one can be sure that despair, not the life of meaning, is the outcome. This fundamental phenomenon is often called the paradox of hedonism—those who aim directly at happiness do not find it; those whose lives have meaning and purpose in duty and responsibility also find happiness.

Perhaps this is where Charlie Brown's Snoopy can give us a lesson in reverse. Snoopy's problem was that he was trying to find happiness in feeling (personal comfort and self-gratification), not in meaning. He kept complaining that life was empty; it had no meaning—until Charlie Brown came in with a bowlful of dog food. Now Snoopy exclaims: "Ah! Meaning." While food and a lot of other things are necessary for survival, they do not necessarily relieve the sense of futility and meaninglessness.

Let's be real—survivors recognize that everyone experiences disappointments and personal failures from time to time. That is, survivors face reality. No one, not even survivors, gets all that he or she hopes for. Varying levels of frustration and defeat dog us all. Most people can handle all this if they belong to caring families or communities. Some close-linked (more primitive!) societies do not know what depression means! In other words, helplessness does not slip into hopelessness if we are connected to others who understand and support us when life tumbles in. But if a warm family circle is missing, if the sense of patriotism in a nation's honor that reflects the highest virtues has faded, if a personal relationship with God no longer matters—then "meaning" is a meaningless word.

What to do about all this? We may not be able to do much about the absence of a traditional family circle. We may not be able to experience a unified nation as, for example, the United States was during World War II. But we can do something about our relationship to the highest Power in the universe—to something larger than we are.

Survivors believe there is meaning to life because God is not only the most powerful Person in the universe, He is also predictable and compassionate. He does not wait for us to discover Him. He is the Hound of heaven. He is the Shepherd of His sheep. He is the Father who has never shut the front door as He waits for us to respond to His appeals to come home. Everyone on this planet feels His tug, His call to fairness and love. The more we permit Him to "speak" to us, either through the Holy Scriptures or through that inner monitor we call conscience, that much more we will sense His presence and involvement in our lives.

Solzhenitsyn, Kornfield, and the Ten Boom sisters discovered this holy Presence in different ways, through different circumstances. But their grasp of meaning found common ground in recognizing that this vast, complicated universe was still, in some way, not out of control. They recognized the personal involvement of God Himself in their lives, miserable as they were.

Further, this personal God wants us to become like Him. That is simply amazing. Only Christianity offers that tremendous truth to human beings.

Where does one learn all this? In the Bible, from Genesis to Revelation. God created this world and declared it very good. Good, that is, until sin entered—that awful word that sums up human rebellion and the clenched fist in the face of God. Read about it in the book of Genesis, preferably in a modern version such as the *Good News Bible* (especially if you are reading Genesis for the first time).

But God did not turn away from people who rebelled. He knew that Satan had much to do with confusing the minds of His creatures. So God continued His relationship with humanity through men and women called "prophets." Such is the core story of the Old Testament.

But the day came when God Himself came to earth on that first Christmas Eve. Unbelievable as it may sound, the story of Jesus of Nazareth is primarily God Himself telling the truth about the way God runs the universe. That is, He is not the kind of person that Satan (and much of humanity) has made Him out to be: He is not severe, unforgiving, harsh, arbitrary, or unfair—all charges made by many of humanity's greatest thinkers through the centuries. Think of the religious systems of the world that operate on the premise that God is arbitrary and severe and must somehow be appeased!

Jesus not only revealed what God is like; He showed us what men and women can be like. He taught us that we can become like Him by the same divine power that enabled Him to be our magnificent pattern and Redeemer. His enduring message is that God is on our side, that love is stronger than death, that struggling for righteousness' sake will be on the daily menu of His followers, and that death is only a sleep—the dead are awaiting His lifegiving call.

That pattern is always the survivor's goal and image to constantly behold. The way Jesus faced up to loneliness, disappointment, and rejection is the path of the survivor today. Fail we may, during our maturing process, but survivors learn through every experience. Their bounce-back power is the open secret; it comes with trusting the long view. That bounce-back power is more than willpower, more than a positive mental attitude. It is the divine energy supplied to those who reach out for God's presence in their lives. That presence, that divine energy, is in reality the Holy Spirit.

The wisest survivors take the longest view of the future. This long view provides calm perspective and the assurance of meaning when the immediate circumstances are tough and forbidding. And this long view grows out of understanding more clearly as time goes by what God has on His mind regarding the future.

In the next chapter we will take a closer look at what God has on His mind regarding the future. We call His unfolding of the future the long view that makes ordinary people into ultimate survivors. Remember, survivors are realists, and only the strong, the prepared, survive.

In summary, survivors survive because they find good reason to persevere. Their reason to persevere explains why hope is so powerful. Furthermore, survivors know their territory in advance, and that reduces anxiety. Some survivors see further into the future because they are listening to the time-tested truths of the Judeo-Christian tradition. Those who see the furthest have discovered good reasons to trust the Creator of the universe, the God whom Jesus came to reveal. Their hearts sing out their appreciation for the cost God has paid for their salvation; their grateful response of trust and obedience is called biblical faith. Any other kind of faith is mere whistling in the dark, or an overdose of self-hypnotism.

So on to the next chapter for a look into the territory that all of us will soon be in.

---

[1] Grand Rapids: Zondervan Publishing House, 1983, pp. 27-34.
[2] New York: Washington Square Press, 1976.
[3] *Ibid.*, p. 5.
[4] *Ibid.*
[5] *The Hiding Place* (Fleming H. Revell Company, 1971), p. 197.
[6] New York: Pocket Books, 1991.
[7] *Ibid.*, p. 287.
[8] *Ibid.*, p. 284.

# Chapter Eleven

# Survivors Know Their Territory

Survivors survive because they have studied the territory that lies ahead. That is one of the basic elements in their ability to survive: they prepare for the known as well as the uncertain. But the uncertain will not be something entirely foreign to the general layout of possibilities that common sense and research can and should provide *today*.

Survivors in life's largest arena are similar to the wise people in Florida who must face the known as well as the uncertain in every hurricane season. We all know of the parable of the wise and the foolish men who built houses on rock and on sand, respectively (see Matt. 7:24-27). The same storm produced survivors and losers. What makes the difference? Listen to the parable of the hurricane:

*The kingdom of survivors is like unto those who hearken diligently to the warnings of the approaching hurricane, preparing their households for its coming fury. The hurricane buildeth in strength in seas afar. Its outstretched arms hurl bullets of rain at awesome speed. Its swirling winds are unmerciful.*

*Whence it cometh and whither it goeth is charted by satellite and measured by instruments precise; those in its path needeth not to be surprised.*

*But many are those who hearken but obey not the warnings. The wind cometh; their homes are not prepared. They are not ready—and the end of them is terrible indeed. But they who take heed unto the warnings save both themselves and their households.*

*They who have ears, let them hear the parable of the hurricane.*

"One man met me at the door of a second-floor apartment with a drink in his hand. Must have been 20 people in there, and I asked all to leave. Another told me that this was his land and if the sheriff wanted him to leave, he'd have to arrest him," related police chief Jerry Peralta of Pass Christian, Mississippi, recalling the fateful evening of August 17, 1969.

"I told them that I couldn't order them out, but I could take from them the names of their next of kin. And that's when they laughed."

For days a hurricane had been building in the Gulf of Mexico, its course and clout calculated by the minute as it gathered extraordinary strength in the warm Gulf. All day long Chief Peralta had sped up and down the highways, stopping at every home, urging everyone to leave immediately. At nightfall, with the storm's winds blowing at 60 miles per hour and the breakers splashing over the seawall, Peralta had decided to make that last call on the hurricane party in the posh Richelieu apartments overlooking the beach.

That night Camille, one of the worst killer storms ever to hit North America, slammed into Mississippi and Louisiana. It blew harder than any hurricane recorded to that time, hurling bullets of rain at 210 miles per hour. It killed 150 people in a single night and smashed property worth well over $1 billion (in 1969 dollars!).

A few hours after the chief left the party at the Richelieu, all the lights and electric power in Pass Christian went out in a single stroke. Fifteen minutes later a giant wave, as high as a three-story house, slammed over the seawall, demolishing everything in its path.

The Richelieu apartments, of steel and concrete, were overwhelmed by the rushing waters and torn to pieces by the ferocious winds. The whole building collapsed in a pile of rubble, killing the 20 people who had gathered for their cozy hurricane party. Twenty people ignored the radio warnings all day long and laughed at the sheriff's last call to flee for their lives.

Will we listen to the parable of the hurricane?

On Monday, August 28, 1979, the hurricane watch center in Miami, Florida, alerted the Caribbean region that tropical storm David had reached hurricane proportions. Throughout that day and Tuesday regular bulletins gave the position of the storm and its direction and intensity, warning that it was developing into the most intense hurricane to threaten the Windward Islands in this century.

At 6:00 Wednesday morning the report specifically indicated that the storm was headed toward Dominica. By 10:00 a.m. David's eye passed over Dominica, and the island will never again be the same. The angry sea, propelling tree trunks and debris as battering rams, scoured the beaches, rearranging them forever. Eyewitnesses compared southern Dominica to Hiroshima after the dropping of the atomic bomb—a brown, bare, destroyed landscape.

Out of a population of 81,000, approximately 60,000 were left homeless, with 37 known dead. More than 90 percent of the island's electrical power had been supplied by hydroelectic plants—they now lay shattered, with ruptured flumes. All electric poles were reported down; restoring electric service would cost an estimated $15 million. Losses from agriculture, the island's main industry, were staggering: bananas, 95 percent; grapefruit, 75 percent; coconuts, 75 percent; limes, 65 percent; other crops, 80 percent. Not for nothing did the Indians of the Guianas call these tropical storms *hyacoran,* or devil; the Haitian Indians use the word *huracan,* meaning evil spirit.

Although the destruction of property was inevitable, was all the loss of life on Dominica necessary? Appallingly, while for days the whole world apprehensively followed the progressive track of the "storm of the century," "the only people who did not seem to be worrying about David were those towards whom it was heading" (*The Bajan and South Caribbean,* October 1979, p. 4).

Precautions on Dominica seemed to have been nonexistent. An indication of this apathy came to light three days after the storm had struck. A leading spokesperson for the Caribbean Development Bank, a resident of Dominica, appeared on Barbados TV to give his account of David's fury. To the astonishment of his audience, he complained that Dominica had not been given enough warning! "Only four hours," he said.

One observer wrote, "The immediate reaction of many viewers was to wonder if Dominicans were living in the same world." After all, neighboring islands had been seeing and hearing about David for at least five days. The same radio broadcasts and TV programs heard and seen by the Barbadians were beamed to Dominica. But somehow Dominicans seemed oblivious to the satellites stationed overhead for the sole purpose of giving that area accurate information about weather changes. The precision information radioed back from the brave pilots of the American reconnaissance aircraft that flew into the eye of David was relayed to Dominica. The continuing drop of the atmospheric pressure, which was an ominous 27.52 inches at noon on Tuesday, should have been warning enough.

During this same period Barbadians feverishly erected storm shelters and nailed up their homes. Businesses on the island shut down, except for the radio station, which continued to give out the latest information, noting the increasing enormity of the danger.

While all this went on in Barbados, Dominica was declaring itself to be only on "hurricane watch" (the lightest of three levels; the others, progressively, are "alert" and "warning"). One Dominican woman interviewed later recalled "that they regarded all this as just another instance of the false alarms they had been given year after year. They were fed up, she said, with rushing to buy food and lanterns at the last minute and then all the paraphernalia of battening down and retiring to their storm cellars, all for nothing" *(ibid.)*.

The report goes on: "In one of the most irresponsible acts of any public service during a national emergency, Radio Dominica went off the air at their scheduled time at 10:00 p.m. Consequently, when at 10:45 on Tuesday night the Barbados Met Office informed their counterparts that David had not only missed Barbados but was then . . . moving dead-on for Dominica, there was no way of informing the Dominican public other than the ancient warning system of ringing the church bells. But even this system seems to have become outmoded in Dominica" *(ibid.)*.

Not until 10:45 a.m. Wednesday was Barbados able to make contact with officialdom in Dominica. Then they were told by the Dominican minister of communication that "the weather had been fine up to eight o'clock that morning and everybody had gone to work as usual. He did however notice that the sky was then overcast and strong winds were already blowing, but it was probably blowing stronger in Martinique. Like a thief in the night, David had crept up on them, Dominicans had opened their doors in the morning to let him in" *(ibid.)*.

For all practical purposes, they refused to be warned. They did not "know" because they refused to hear.

Will we learn the lesson of the parable of the hurricane? Ultimate survivors will.

Another storm, greater than Camille or David or Andrew, is soon to break over Planet Earth. The Bible calls it the seven last plagues, culminating in Armageddon and "a time of trouble, such as never has been since there was a nation till that time" (Dan. 12:1, RSV).

But before this storm breaks, God will have given a worldwide message to prepare for the worst. No one will ever look back and say that he or she never heard the warning. Do you know what that message says? Survivors will know!

Jesus likened this coming storm and warning message to the days of Noah. When we talk about the storm in Noah's day, we are talking about a big-league storm—a storm so big, so global, so final, so unrelenting in its fury, that the whole civilized world was flooded and no one survived except those who responded to God's warning message (see Genesis 6-8). There is something very final about laughing at one's last warning to prepare for the coming storm.

In Matthew 24 Jesus says: "As were the days of Noah, so will be the coming of the Son of man. For as in those days before the flood they were eating and drinking, marrying and giving in marriage, until the day when Noah entered the ark, and they did not know until the flood came and swept them all away, so will be the coming of the Son of man" (verses 37-39, RSV).

What could Jesus mean—"they did not know"? After all, Noah had been warning his world for 120 years. He had built an enormous boat that had become the butt of ridicule for more than a century! Noah had been front-page news for years, until his boat and message became old news. This was the way the Dominicans felt about David—the same old story, again and again.

Noah and his family were survivors—supersurvivors! What kept them going? What kind of message did they preach? And what kind of man was Noah that God could entrust to him such an important assignment?

Noah was a prototype of the survivors who live in these last days. We read in Genesis 6:9: "Noah was a righteous man, blameless in his generation; Noah walked with God" (RSV). He had all the marks of a survivor before he began building that ark!

His message, Peter tells us, was clear and uncompromising: Noah was a "preacher of righteousness" (2 Peter 2:5). Why was this important? Take a look at Noah's world, a world that had lost its grip on morality and fidelity—a world in which righteousness was almost extinguished.

The record states that "the Lord saw that the wickedness of man was great in the earth, and that every imagination of the thoughts of his heart was only evil continually" (Gen. 6:5, RSV). "And God saw the earth, and behold, it was corrupt; for all flesh had corrupted their way upon the earth" (verse 12).

"As were the days of Noah, so will be the coming of the Son of man" (Matt. 24:37, RSV). What is Jesus saying? The entire chapter is focused on Jesus' answer to the question "What will be the sign of your coming and of the close of the age?" (verse 3, RSV). One of His chief points was that the good news that He had come to earth to make clear—the gospel—"will be preached throughout the whole world, as a testimony to all nations; and then the end will come" (verse 14, RSV).

A few verses later Jesus directs His hearers to Noah so that they all can learn the lesson of the prototype survivor. The storm that precedes His second coming will even surpass the Flood in Noah's day; it will involve people all over the world, far more than in Noah's day. But the issues will be the same, and the end is as sure. In these last days, as in Noah's day, God would have everyone enter the "ark." He will see to it that His everlasting gospel will go clearly to all the world before Christ Jesus returns. And the message that people hear will be an appeal to righteousness. Even as Noah preached the message of hope, cheer, and righteousness in a very bleak time, so God will have a people proclaiming worldwide that same message—a "call for the endurance of the saints, those who keep the commandments of God and the faith of Jesus" (Rev. 14:12, RSV). More about that message in the next chapter.

But what about that territory of the last days that survivors will plan for? What will conditions be like during those increasingly worldwide tensions? Do we really need to elaborate on any comparison between Noah's day and ours? It seems so obvious!

In earlier chapters we touched on some of the concerns that men and women are facing today. For many people, the year 2000 and beyond brings many of those worries into sharp focus. Survivors prepare, but not in fear. Fear is a negative emotion that temporarily stops a particular action, but fear cannot be relied upon to induce a positive change. God, at times, has presented fearful alternatives as He has appealed to people to consider their ways. But His main emphasis has been the positive appeal, fleshed out with love and grace.

That's why Noah and last-day proclaimers of "the end" appeal to contemporaries to look up, to respond to God's invitation to live righteously (that is, "right-wisely"), to endure under tough times, and to become comfortable with "the commandments of God and the faith of Jesus." In other words, the appeal is to be real survivors.

Our second observation: Noah's generation (which mirrors the "last" generation) "did not know" (Matt. 24:39, RSV). Really? What did they not know? They thought they knew more than Noah did! They "knew" (that is, they thought they knew), on the basis of anything they had seen or heard, that there was no reason to expect doom. True, the world was a mess, society was in constant stress, and strife characterized the political world. Just like many in Dominica and Pass Christian, Mississippi, who laughed off the warnings before David and Camille slammed into them—"We've heard all this before. What's new?"

And that is the point! In recent years old and young have become used to tensions and the degrading of lifestyles until what was unspeakable in the parents' generation becomes common talk on prime-time TV for their children. Compare the past 30 years and how societies everywhere have defined down not only deviancy but also offensiveness. It is chilling to have children even hear the latest news broadcasts! But we muddle through somehow, and our fears and disgust are soon forgotten. For Noah's generation, in spite of all the moral darkness, *the future looked bright because their religious leaders, scientists, and educational leaders said it would be!*

"So it will be" in the last days before Jesus returns.

The same Jesus who lived, died, and was resurrected pleads with us today with the same intensity that compelled Noah to preach his "offbeat" message. To us in our day, genuine survivors will listen carefully. They won't trust their own instincts or the pronouncements of worldly-wise thinkers. They keep their focus by repeating often those words of Jesus: "So it will be."

Survivors will repeat the Lord's words in the face of the scoffers when Peter's prediction comes true: "Scoffers will come in the last days with scoffing, following their own passions and saying, "Where is the promise of his coming?" (2 Peter 3:3, 4, RSV). Then Peter reminds his readers that that is what was said in Noah's day prior to the Flood.

All this leads to our third observation, which will add to the framework of a real survivor's thinking. Those who are concerned exclusively with pessimistic predictions regarding the state of the world before probation closes (which will occur a short time before Jesus returns) will be disappointed and will probably be just as lost as those who scoffed at Noah. They didn't respond genuinely to the message of "righteousness."

My favorite author put it this way: "Come when it may, the day of God will come unawares to the ungodly. When life is going on in its unvarying round; when men are absorbed in pleasure, in business, in traffic, in money-making; when religious leaders are magnifying the world's progress and enlightenment, and the people are lulled in a false security—then, as the midnight thief steals within the unguarded dwelling, so shall sudden destruction come upon the careless and ungodly "and they shall not escape" (1 Thess. 5:3).[1]

In other words, those unprepared for the close of probation will not "know" the truth about transpiring events, *because they refuse to know.* They prefer to "know" (or believe) what best supports their personal desires and selfish ambitions. The worldly-wise will "know" only what coincides with their presuppositions.

But survivors have learned to look at *all* the evidence; they recognize that human predictions about the future have generally been very wrong. They have learned to trust the God of the universe, who is both predictable and compassionate. And what He has said about how evil, sin, and suffering will finally be destroyed makes sense to genuine survivors.

All this leads to our next observation: Just as world conditions prior to the Flood did not compel people to believe that the end was near, so world conditions prior to the close of probation and before the seven last plagues will not give the last generation indisputable and direct evidence that the end is near.

It is the paradox of horror on one hand and the asphyxiating optimism in the face of reality on the other. After living through decades of unprecedented global horror, after teetering for years on the brink of nuclear disaster, numb with statistics describing millions living on a starvation level or plagued by pollution disasters—more of the same only seems to anesthetize further our sensibilities. We find ourselves flipping the TV channels or turning the pages of newspapers, each full of incredible disaster horror somewhere, as if horror is as normal as the weather report.

Ironically, prospects of a peaceful, pleasant world may be more promising and believable for those living just before the close of probation than at any other time in world history. If the world appears on the verge of removing dreadful physical diseases (when was the last time you saw a polio patient?), pollution problems (many of the lakes and rivers in North America are much cleaner than 50 years ago), hunger and poverty, as well as establishing an unprecedented world peace organization—will not dire warnings of the end of the world seem as unreal and unbelievable as the words of lonely Noah must have seemed when he implored his neighbors to enter the ark? "As it was in the days of Noah . . ."

No question about it, troubles will be rampant and electronically presented before most families throughout the world in living color on the 6:00 p.m. news. But the paradox of horror will prevail. Although troubles in natural disasters and social unrest can be expected on an increasingly greater scale, we have developed an enormous capacity to adjust to such troubles.

Furthermore, in the spirit of it all, men and women seem profoundly eager to believe that technology will unfailingly come up with whatever is necessary to eventually wipe out all such causes for anxiety. No wonder Ellen White could write that probation will close "when religious leaders are magnifying the world's progress and enlightenment," when "all are looking forward to many years of worldly prosperity."[2]

Throughout the Bible we see the interplay of Satan as he tries to thwart God's plan for saving men and women out of this world and into the next. These men and women will be safe to save; rebellion, sin, and death will not arise again. Those people are the ultimate survivors; they are the reason the universe will once again be secure from evil. They have permitted God to help them develop character patterns (sufficient boutons) that will never again say no to His way of running the universe.

Thus it is no small wonder that Satan will so arrange matters that this world, amidst all its "normal" tensions and sinking moral decadence, will be deceived and preoccupied as the end draws on. He will not play into God's hands, any more than he did in Noah's day, by permitting society to fall apart drastically or by manipulating the forces of nature so that this planet appears about to destroy itself. He will play the game of balancing off whatever is intrinsically bad with plausible, enthralling prospects of an improving world amid its growing pains. "As it was in the days of Noah . . ."

---

[1] Ellen G. White, *The Great Controversy* (Boise, Idaho: Pacific Press Pub. Assn., 1911), p. 38. See also p. 338.

[2] *Ibid.*, pp. 38, 338.

# Chapter Twelve

# Survivors Trust the Long View

On October 12, 1992, the 500th anniversary of Columbus' landing on islands in the New World, NASA scientists wanted to commemorate that event with their own exploration—but this time it would be the universe! They simultaneously turned on two of the world's most powerful radio telescopes, one in California and the other in Puerto Rico. Each dish is 1,000 feet wide and 167 feet deep in the center.

What were they looking for? They wanted to know if intelligent beings live elsewhere in the universe. They continue to analyze all microwave signals by computer, billions and billions of signals that normally hit this planet every day. Out of this daily analysis, which has already cost $100 million, they hope to find a radio message from an intelligent creature far out in space.

But one does not need to search microwaves for a message from space. Messages have been coming since the creation of this world. John the revelator, for one, has given us a remarkable picture of three angels who fly "in the midst of heaven" with a message for all the world to hear before the end of time (Rev. 14:6-12). These angels are depicted as working through men and women to give God's last call to men and women before probation closes, as we noted in the previous chapter.

Ultimate survivors take these messages very seriously. They study carefully the description of those who will respond to these messages. That description is found in Revelation 14 immediately before the messages of the three angels.

Ultimate survivors have their "Father's name written on their foreheads" (verse 1, RSV). What's in a name, in a signature? Many products are bought primarily on the strength of a product's endorsers or a famous signature. Ask any art collector or clock collector. Ask any world-class violinist as he or she checks their Stradivarius. Ask any young man or woman when they buy Arnold Palmer or Tiger Wood golf clubs or Chris Evert tennis rackets. Or look around at the Cardin shirts or Dior ties or Gucci handbags and shoes.

For many products, the name means almost everything. It means that the product carries the endorsement of someone who cares about quality, someone who can be trusted. If Arnold Palmer has his signature on those golf clubs, they must be the best! Those names in all the advertisements around the world, for anything from athletic shoes to washing machines, mean quality, that you can trust the products that those names are on.

Remember those TV ads for Hanes underclothing? I can still see that determined inspector, with all her formidable charm, overseeing the assembly line, checking the finished products, and saying: "The quality goes in before the name goes on."

The ultimate survivors are also described in Revelation 7 as those who are "sealed . . . in their foreheads." The sealing and God's name in the forehead symbolize that ultimate survivors are sealed with God's approval. Many products can't be sold without a valid seal of approval, the seal that tells the world that the product has passed the tests of reliability. Note that yellow Underwriter's Seal on the bottom of electrical appliances, or such valid endorsements as the Good Housekeeping Seal of Approval or the seal of *Parent's Magazine* on baby items.

This is what God is telling the universe when He seals His faithful survivors with His signature in their foreheads: "Listen to these survivors. Watch them handle tough times. You can trust them. I can stamp them with My seal of approval. The quality has gone in before My name went on!"

Another distinguishing mark of these survivors is that they "follow the Lamb [Jesus] wherever he goes" (Rev. 14:4, RSV). As we have noted in these pages, survivors make a habit of taking the long view. Further, they have made a habit of plugging in to that Power that has proved reliable in maintaining a hopeful, persevering spirit. These ultimate survivors have discovered that the biblical view of humanity's predicament and future makes more sense than anything else; they have discovered through experience that the Lord of the Bible reaches into their lives with hope and power, and helps them to endure to the end. Yes, for them it is their highest joy and privilege to "follow the Lamb wherever he goes."

A further mark of these ultimate survivors is that they are men and women of integrity; no "guile" is found in them. Why this unadorned characteristic? Why didn't John simply say, "They are full of love"? The message is that the "redeemed from the earth" (verse 3) have, by God's help, overcome in their own experience the killer virus that started the cosmic conflict long before this world was created—deceit, guile, dissembling. Such was the core mark of Lucifer or Satan, the author of sin, suffering, and death (see John 8:44; Rev. 12:9).

No more double entendres, no more winks that belie the words, no more whispers of faint praise running contrary to one's real meaning, no more promises without fidelity. These survivors are safe to save because they can be trusted. All through their earthly lives they developed a spontaneous habit of telling the truth. They were truthful with themselves and with others, especially when tempted to turn from known duty, just as Boris Kornfield would not bend when asked to commit another prisoner to his death in solitary confinement.

Now, those three messages (Rev. 14:6-12) that last-day survivors heard clearly, what did they say?

The first angel proclaims "the everlasting gospel" in a worldwide assignment. No local affair, no special group! Nobody will be left out. In some way, all people of the world will hear enough about the gospel to make an intelligent decision that will direct the rest of their lives.

What is that gospel? The same message that Jesus proclaimed: "Repent, and believe in [have faith in] the gospel" (Mark 1:15, RSV). When anyone is in doubt regarding the gospel, or confused by the jungle of theological discussion, go back to the words of Jesus. Jesus is the gospel, the best good news that this world has ever seen or heard. Whatever He said or did is "good news"!

The gospel is the "old, old story" of how "God so loved the world that He gave His only begotten Son, that whoever believes [has faith] in Him should not perish but have everlasting life. For God did not send His Son into the world to condemn the world, but that the world through Him might be saved" (John 3:16, 17, NKJV).

The gospel is the old, but ever new, good news that God not only has never shut His front door but is reaching out constantly through His Holy Spirit to lead people back home. I am not talking in mysteries or riddles or in romantic language. God does speak, in some way, to every man, woman, and child. He wants survivors from this messy world who are, by His help, without guile—people who love spontaneously, people who can bear His endorsement that they can be trusted.

The dramatic focus for this wonderful story (the gospel) is Jesus on that Roman cross, strung up to die as a criminal because powerful men and women could not handle His picture of God, so contrary to the religions and philosophies of the world. But He turned the cross of shame into the pulpit of the universe. He said: "I, if I am lifted up from the earth, will draw all peoples to Myself" (John 12:32, NKJV).

Something about that cross gets inside of those who stop and look. He is the Creator, dying for His creation. But this "dying" is far more than only physical shame and horrible torture. He was not merely "lent" to this world for 33 years. Forever the Creator has locked Himself into time and space, forever to live within a human body. Forever He will be the constant reminder that God will truly go to the "uttermost" (Heb. 7:25) to reconcile rebels unto Himself. In a profound way, beyond words, Jesus died for *you and me.*

But there is something that accompanies this "everlasting gospel." That is the urgency of the three messages. With a "loud voice" the first angel proclaims to the world that it is judgment time—"the hour of His judgment has come" (Rev. 14:7, NJKV).

Judgment time! We can understand it in two ways: (1) judgment time for men and women, and (2) judgment time for God! That's right; John says that the hour of God's judgment has come! The whole story from Genesis to Revelation, from Creation to the end of this world when Jesus returns, focuses on the cosmic conflict, the great controversy, between God and Satan. And now, judgment time!

Satan has misrepresented God as being severe, unforgiving, harsh, and arbitrary, exactly his own characteristics. The main issue has been, Who could run the universe best, God or Satan? Did God make rules that created beings could not keep, especially if they wanted to be happy and free individuals? In other words, is God unfair to judge men and women for breaking laws that could not be kept?

The biblical story reveals how that controversy has been playing out through the years. And it tells us how the story winds up. The first angel's message proclaims that the time has come for a review of the evidence—in the days just before the return of Jesus. The redeemed of earth, the ultimate survivors, will eventually sing out in one voice: "Alleluia! Salvation and glory and honor and power belong to the Lord our God! For true and righteous are His judgments" (Rev. 19:1, 2, NJKV).

One of the strongest evidences for the fairness of God in the "hour of His judgment" is the emergence of those survivors who in the last days "follow the Lamb wherever he goes," people who are endorsed by God Himself as people who can be trusted. In fact, the third angel describes these survivors who rightly represent God this way: "This calls for endurance on the part of God's people, those who obey God's commandments and are faithful to Jesus" (Rev. 14:12, TEV).

Again listen to the first angel: "Fear God and give glory to Him, for the hour of His judgment has come; and worship Him who made heaven and earth" (verse 7, NKJV). Here is God's description of how He will come out looking right in the "hour of His judgment": His friends, the ultimate survivors, will make God look good and exonerated when they "give glory to Him" through their words and actions. They are without "guile," they are comfortable with His commandments, and they are glad to "worship Him who made heaven and earth."

In other words, God is judged not to be the kind of person Satan has made Him out to be. He makes His case, not through shouting out His defense, not even by attacking Satan for his lies, not by coercion of any kind on anybody, but by telling His story we call the gospel. Those men and women who trust His story discover that God's promises are as reliable as the rising sun, that people who follow Him wherever He goes eventually become people without guile, trustworthy, and loving beyond measure. This kind of human response is what the Bible calls giving "glory" to God.

Ultimate survivors have discovered that the Creator-God, not the philosophical constructs that picture God as the Unmoved Mover, or the Spirit of the Universe, or the Angry Judge, or the Cosmic Policeman, or the Force, is not someone to be afraid of but Someone to worship. The judgment is not a scary event; the judgment is good news because the universe has seen that God's plan for redeeming the world from its rebelling mess truly works—look at the kind of people it develops! The judgment declares that God is good and that His commandments are right, fair, and reasonable.

How about that second angel, the dire pronouncement that "Babylon is fallen, . . . that great city, because she has made all nations drink of the wine of the wrath of her fornication" (verse 8, NKJV)?

Who or what is Babylon? The Old Testament records a list of enemies who tried to destroy the Jews, but the mother of all enemies was Babylon. Babylonians destroyed Jerusalem and the sacred Temple; they ravished the land and dispersed the Jews throughout their widespread empire. But even more important, Babylon represented a counterfeit religion that has had pervasive influence through the centuries.

When John used the term *Babylon,* he combined in that term both the perverted religious system and the coercive power that well-nigh obliterated ancient Israel. In the last days, John is saying, a worldwide religious system possessing coercive power will again attempt to unify the world into one religious voice.

Revelation 13 foretells the universal appeal and strength of that religious power in the last days that will "cause as many as would not worship the image of the beast to be killed" (verse 15, NKJV). Revelation 17 and 18 develop further details regarding the enormous power and appeal of Babylon. Babylon in the end-times signifies any and all religions that promise salvation by any other means than character transformation that brings "glory" to God. But like ancient Babylon, modern last-day Babylon will form a world confederacy of religious and political powers that will try to destroy those who "keep the commandments of God, and the faith of Jesus" (Rev. 14:12).

In the last days ultimate survivors in all religious groups will finally draw their personal line in the sand; the issues will be clear-cut. More and more they will have seen the implications and consequences of following the persuasive appeal of Babylon. They see more clearly the deceptive weakness in that basic appeal—the promise of eternal life without a change in character. They reject the easy "gospel" that focuses primarily on forgiveness rather than a forgiveness that opens the door to the joy of a new birth and a restoration of life that conforms to the will of God. That is why Babylon is always furious with those who welcome God's promise to help ultimate survivors "keep the commandments of God, and the faith of Jesus" (Rev. 14:12).

Eventually the time comes when survivors everywhere respond to the call: "Come out of her, my people, lest you share in her sins, and lest you receive of her plagues" (Rev. 18:4, NKJV). These people are the ultimate survivors who have listened and responded to the second angel's message of Revelation 14.

The third, and final, angel is blunt and nonnegotiable: "If anyone worships the beast and his image, and receives his mark on his forehead or on his hand [see Revelation 13:15, 16], he himself shall also drink of the wine of the wrath of God, which is poured out full strength into the cup of His indignation. . . . Here is the patience of the saints; here are those who keep the commandments of God and the faith of Jesus" (Rev. 14:9-12, NKJV).

What could all this mean? Is there any good news in the third angel's message? The good news is that we can trust the God who is running the universe. We live in a predictable universe; ideas and actions do have consequences. The apostle Paul said it clearly: "Do not be deceived, God is not mocked; for whatever a man sows, that he will also reap" (Gal. 6:7, NKJV).

The awful consequences of rebelling against the wisdom of God—selfishness and covetousness, as seen in rape, murder, hate, deceit, war, poverty—will finally play out in the moral meltdown in the last days. Sin destroys anyone who refuses to stop rebelling.

The survivor has learned that by merely looking around. Tobacco kills, arsenic kills, hate kills, unfulfilled gratifications kill, dishonesty leads to self-defense and worse.

In other words, rebellion against the Creator of the universe has serious and everlasting consequences. Not because God has been miffed and will get even. Hardly! Sinners reap what they have sown. Just as the law of gravity can be trusted, and functions regardless of one's personal opinion, so the law of cause and effect can be trusted; it has nothing to do with how people "feel" about that law. The law of cause and effect is one of the most powerful reasons for trusting the wisdom and love of God. The only reason this world has not collapsed in a moral meltdown is that God has had His restraining influence on men and women who have not yet fully committed themselves, either to be commandment keepers or to worship the beast/Babylon. But that fateful moment is coming when God finally leaves men and women to live out their strongest desires, for good or ill, without the Holy Spirit's restraining influence. We call that moment the close of probation, occurring prior to the seven last plagues.

The Bible story is consistent, affirming that the wicked will finally be destroyed. The greatest suffering of the wicked will be their final anguish when they recall, like an endless tape, when and where they had resisted grace and love, time and again. That mental tape will roll on until that fateful moment when they finally tuned out the Spirit once for all. Of course, Satan will suffer the longest and the worst of all.

We all know something now of that relationship between sin and unrest—we have all been there. Isaiah said it well: "The wicked are like the troubled sea, when it cannot rest, whose waters cast up mire and dirt. 'There is no peace,' says my God, 'for the wicked'" (Isa. 57:20, 21, NKJV). But Satan has had this "unrest," growing to monstrous proportions, ever since his original break with his Creator at the beginning of the tragic conflict. And his suffering at the end will become more intense than anyone can imagine as he recognizes finally that his terrible experiment with rebellion was a colossal failure. That truly is hell.

But the law of cause and effect has its bright side. For example, we learned in chapter 5 that a proper diet and exercise will ensure a life free from most physical diseases. Survivors have learned that high purpose and achievement depend on keeping both short- and long-range goals in clear view. It is a law that can be trusted. The law of cause and effect operates on all levels of life.

That is why ultimate survivors keep adjusting the long view into sharper focus. They keep clarifying where they want to be 5,000 years from now, not just five years from now. The issues become increasingly transparent, the outcomes of choices are as clear as the noonday sun.

Ultimate survivors relate to their friendly Creator as the wise sailor relates to the lighthouse. They trust Him as a powerful, predictable, compassionate God. They have learned through experience that God provides great reasons to hope in times of perplexity. Further, survivors have learned that God provides the spiritual strength to endure while they hope.

In taking the long look into the future, survivors recognize that any life after death would have to be on God's terms, not theirs. They further recognize that God has been very specific about the kind of people who ultimately survive their human probationary period. They do not confuse God's love with His approval, nor do they think tolerance and fairness are synonymous.

Survivors take seriously the various descriptions biblical writers have made regarding those who live forever: "Do you not know that the unrighteous will not inherit the kingdom of God? Do not be deceived. Neither fornicators, nor idolaters, nor adulterers, nor homosexuals, nor sodomites, nor thieves, nor covetous, nor drunkards, nor revilers, nor extortioners will inherit the kingdom of God. And such were some of you" (1 Cor. 6:9-11, NKJV).

John wrote a similar description: "He who overcomes shall inherit all things, and I will be his God and he shall be My son. But the cowardly, unbelieving, abominable, murderers, sexually immoral, sorcerers, idolaters, and all liars shall have their part in the lake which burns with fire and brimstone, which is the second death" (Rev. 21:7, 8, NKJV).

Ultimate survivors, however, don't focus on negatives. They realize that they have been trusting the long view and the God whose reputation guarantees that view. They know that they are still maturing; they trust the God about whom it was said: "I am sure that God, who began this good work in you, will carry it on until it is finished" (Phil. 1:6, TEV).

In New York Harbor, less than two miles from

Manhattan, is Liberty Island and one of the largest statues in the world. We call that copper lady the Statue of Liberty. About 2 million people visit her annually.

Since 1886 she has been the first sight of the New World for millions of immigrants pouring into New York City. Many of these millions could not speak the language of America. But they knew what that lady was saying to them. Their last hope was America, and that statue seemed to say it all as it guided their ship to freedom and a new life.

On the base of the statue are words that sum up all this unspeakable hope. Read these words, written by Emma Lazarus, as if you were in those boats, breathing freedom for the first time:

> "Give me your tired, your poor,
> Your huddled masses yearning to breathe free,
> The wretched refuse of your teeming shore.
> Send these, the homeless, tempest-tost to me.
> I lift my lamp beside the golden door!"

Survivors understand these words now, but never more clearly than when they eventually step into the new earth. Sooner or later they discover that their best thoughts and their best actions were developed while they focused on their highest duties and their warmest intimations to love and serve others. In addition, if they were fortunate enough to learn about Jesus Christ in their earthly lives, He became their pattern and guide, their model and pathfinder. They kept their eyes on the lifted-up Jesus Christ—the Light of the universe, the Light that will never go out, the Light they had learned to trust when all other lights flickered or failed.

This Light stands in front of that one golden door in that one harbor in all the universe that puts to rest every human anxiety, assuages every grief, and rekindles every junked dream. That golden door leads to God's plan for your future. That Light will be all we need to find that door.

Like the Great Lady in New York Harbor, our Lord's arms are outstretched to you and to me, calling as He waits: "Come to me, all of you who are tired from carrying heavy loads, and I will give you rest. Take my yoke and put it on you, and learn from me, because I am gentle and humble in spirit; and you will find rest" (Matt. 11:28, 29, TEV).

The good news about final events is that God will step into the human fray and take charge. One of these days the eastern sky will brighten as we have never seen it before; we will hear trumpets like we have never heard music. Grassy plots all over this planet will break open, the oceans will give up their dead as boys and girls, fathers and mothers, hear the voice of the Life-giver.

All of us are looking forward to seeing those smiling faces of those who have been sleeping for a while. A lot of tired bodies now gone will walk and run again. Many children will be led by angels to their parents to be cuddled again. Millions of spiritual heroes, the ultimate survivors—especially those many who were killed for their faithfulness to Jesus—will finally be compensated. And some mother, some father, some son or daughter, some friend, some lover, will be looking for you. A place with your name on it is set at the great supper.

At the great "marriage supper of the Lamb [Jesus]" (see Rev. 19:9) all the ultimate survivors will find their name card and their chair at the table. Loved ones and friends of many centuries will sit down at last, without a thought about former anxieties.

But not all is joy. These same loved ones and friends will go up and down that table looking for a particular name, a special chair. Fathers will look for their wonderful sons, mothers will seek the daughter who was a dream come true. Brothers will look for each other, sisters will listen for that familiar laugh. But not every place will be filled with those who started out well. Only those who kept their eyes on their Leader, following Him wherever He led them—survivors in whom there was no guile—will be the ultimate survivors.

The unavoidable question remains: Will you follow on, following Him wherever He may lead you? Will you be found at your chair in the marriage supper of the Lamb? Ultimate survivors will be there. All of them! Let's look for each other!

**Project Sunlight**

June Strong's gripping story about what it could be like in the final days just before Jesus comes again provides a moving illustration of God's tender concern for His children. Paperback, 128 pages. US$1.99, Can$2.99.

**Sixty Ways to Energize Your Life**

Here you'll find 60 ways to boost your spiritual, physical, and mental health. Authored by health professionals and inspirational writers, this book will bring you closer to God and help you learn to honor Him through healthy choices. Compiled by Jan W. Kuzma, Kay Kuzma, and DeWitt S. Williams. Paperback, 128 pages. US$2.49, Can$3.69.

**Thirteen Life-changing Secrets**

Mark Finley, host of the popular TV program *It Is Written,* shares Bible secrets that can make an exciting difference in your life. Discover the peace of forgiveness, the joy of Sabbath rest, the promise of heaven, the power of prayer, and special Bible truths for today. Paper, 122 pages. US$1.99, Can$2.99.

**Your Bible and You**

Arthur S. Maxwell's popular explanation of Bible truths has been a best-seller for 30 years. His crystal-clear explanations will give you new understandings of what the Bible says and its meaning for your life. Paper, 254 pages. US$2.99, Can$4.49.

**To order, call 1-800-765-6955.**